AFTER THE GREAT
TRAGEDY

AFTER THE GREAT
TRAGEDY

J. G. BRACO

First U.S. edition 2013

Copyright © 2001 Josip Grbavac

Published in the United States by
Awakening Within
Kealakekua, Hawaii 96750

The original title in Croatian:
NAKON VELIKE TRAGEDIJE

First published in Croatian in 2001 by
Budenje, Ltd., Zagreb, Croatia

The CIP Number in the online catalog of the University of
Zagreb Library is under the Number 785435

English edition:
Translated by Milosh Zezelj, Nenad Zezelj, Julie Tu
Editor: Angelika Whitecliff
Copy Editor: Christy Walker

Library of Congress Control Number: 2013948899

ISBN: 978-0-9842970-1-6

Printed in the United States of America

CONTENTS

PREFACE

First of all, I want to say that my editor deserves the credit for the publication of this book. After repeatedly and relentlessly talking to me for a long time, he successfully convinced me that it would be of interest both to the people who come to see me, as well as to a wider audience. So finally I agreed and went to work, and this book was created by linking together my previous books, *The Awakening* and *The Sun*.

But neither *The Awakening* nor *The Sun* was written following my decision to do so. Furthermore, I didn't know what I was going to write when I started writing. I would say that I don't directly have anything to do with the writing of these books. You may ask how this is possible, but it is possible. One can imagine it as entering a room and turning on the light. The room is illuminated because a bulb is lit. And I'm like that bulb that you perceive.

For this bulb to be lit and shine, a number of complex conditions must be met. Primarily, the available switch is necessary for the light to be lit, but someone has to press that switch on so that the light will shine. Here the same goes for me. Suddenly, as if I am being switched on, an unexplainable energy guides me, but without my knowing exactly what, or how much I will write. The only thing I know is that I can give thanks to our dear Ivica for this strange energy. As always, his strength affects me the same way as it will all of you, my dear friends and readers.

Even though I have to thank Ivica for everything I have written, now that he is not physically among us, I am aware of my higher responsibility for everything that I do as well as for all that I write. Everything I've written so far was done on the main desk in our office at Srebrnjak Street No. 1. How do I work, and do the people outside in the waiting room know that a new book is being written? There are usually up to 30 people in the waiting room expecting to see me. Not one of them, and not even my closest colleagues know that "it has started" again, for it starts unexpectedly, spontaneously.

I will describe such a situation: I woke up one morning in spring, as usual around 6 o'clock in the morning. I looked out of the window and was glad to see the sun. I was feeling happy without even knowing the reason why. But apparently, my angel was already guiding me. Damir used to pick me up every morning, but that morning I decided to go alone to Srebrnjak 1. I set off, but some inner voice told me, *Go to Maksimir Park.*

So I headed through the Maksimir woods, and when I reached the third lake, I was feeling exceptional happiness. Half an hour later I arrived to our office at Srebrnjak 1. With devotion and total tranquility, I calmly dedicated myself to the usual preparations of the day. I opened a letter that I had received the previous day for my birthday with a certain automatism. It contained the following poem:

When I die and the air of April
places its heavy soaked hair over my grave,
bending over me—if you suffer,
I will no longer love you,
I will be calm like the crown of a tree,
with its relaxed branches when the rain is falling,
quieter and of a harder heart than you now will I be.

When I die
and when I stop hating myself
my love, my dear consolation,
tell me, what should I leave you?
Would you perhaps want eternity?
Or a thousand floral paths?
But there are too many thorns in the flowers,
And eternity has no road signs.

Do you want a pocketful of happiness for all those

unsaved?
Do you want my verses that were written a long, long
time ago?
Maybe you want a tiny bit of the sky, blue like blue silk.
Let it remind you that I am no longer there,
but that I was.

When I finished reading, an inner voice spoke to me and said, *A new book!* Oh God, it had started, I thought to myself, *How, right now at Srebrnjak 1?* But people are waiting here for me, how can I write now? But the voice said: *Don't make excuses. Sit down, take a pencil and leave the rest to us.* It was 8:22 a.m., and there were 30 people in the waiting room.

So you see, if you think that I decide what and when I am going to write, then you are hugely mistaken. This book of mine, like all the others, was born here, at Srebrnjak 1. And I write them bit by bit, adding something in the pauses between every group session. I don't know how much longer this will be going on in this way. Wish me a lot of luck, because I too expect as much as you do. I would be glad if you like this book as well. I worked on it with this assurance, and the proof that I was right will come after you read it.

Josip Grbavac ~ Braco

Part I

THE AWAKENING

1

THE ROAD TO ETERNITY

I feel that you, like me, cannot believe that our beloved Ivica is gone. We cannot see his physical body anymore, but he is still with us.

If someone were to ask me how I feel, I would simply answer, "strange." It is as if he is sitting next to me and telling me what to write. Today is Friday, May 5, 1995. It is 12:20 p.m. No, I didn't know that I was going to write this book. I am doing this because an invisible energy is pushing me, and the pencil, as if moving on its own, is creating a letter, a word, a sentence.

Now I remember an experience that I had with Ivica. He and I, as well as Damir and Dinko, were driving in a car. Ivica explained something to us and suddenly screamed, "My dear Braco, if you knew what awaits you!" And I asked very ingenuously:

"What is awaiting me? I know that I will always be with you and that you will take care of it all."

He smiled and said: "My son, you are still young and don't know anything. You are still in retirement, but when you begin to work, I wouldn't wish to be in your skin." Dinko, Damir and I looked at each other confused, not saying anything. Then Ivica said: "Soon you will grow up, but until then, I have to take care of you. I've been waiting for you since I was 17 years old. Do you think that I have wanted this? No, I was the one who least wanted it. But what can I do? I only follow orders. I wish you had remained where you were. You have a high university education, you are handsome, you have money, but apparently I can't judge you. Soon the time will come when you will be the one writing the books."

At that point I didn't want to hear anymore, and I started yelling: "What are you talking about? What books? You are here to write the books. Mr. Prokic, I beg you, don't get angry, but I don't understand a word that you are saying to me. This cannot happen; I don't want it." But he only smiled and said: "It's fine, my son, we shall see, but you have to understand that you still are a baby and that you don't know anything." I thought, *Oh God, how am I a baby when I'm 26 years old?* Answering my question, he said: "Yes, you are 26 years old, but in reality you are like a 7-year-old child."

If you're wondering if I understood anything he said back then, nothing at all; but now, some things more. Through luck, Dinko and Damir were in the car with us when Ivica proclaimed these words, so they can confirm this. And like all the other prophecies of Ivica, this one was also fulfilled. That is how this first book begins. I write alone, but this is nonsense. Actually, where could this knowledge come from without anyone telling me what to write? This book, in reality, is the continuation of what our beloved and always present Ivica began.

The tragic event took place on April 23, 1995, at about 11:00 a.m. in the Republic of South Africa. Ivica drowned on the coast of the Indian Ocean. No one can believe such a thing happened, so I will explain the sequence of events exactly as they occurred.

In November 1994, we made a tour through Germany. Ivica had been scheduling tours through Germany every month, so nothing of special note attracted our attention at first. He received a group of 50 firstcomers, and suddenly a charming, relatively tall and handsomely built gentleman caught his attention. Ivica shouted: "You, standing over there, I know that you don't believe in anything and that you're here to make fun of me. But know that you will come back again. You suffer from a grave illness. The doctors have told you that there's no cure for you. This is your last stop, and know that you will return." The young gentleman left, but none of this would be important if that same gentleman, whose name was Nenad, hadn't come back, as he was told he would. Yes, he returned. Not immediately, but the next month during the following tour.

Ivica said: "Here, you have come! And surely you thought you would not come back again. My son, listen to me now: Without any help, you would not have come. And now, you tell the people of what you have suffered."

The gentleman said in front of the crowd: "Folks, this is the truth. This man is not a common and ordinary man. Who he is, I don't know, but I know that he sees and knows everything. He is incapable of being lied to. I suffered from cancer and I have visited many doctors in Switzerland, Germany and South Africa. All of them told me that there was no cure for me. Mr. Prokic asked me how much money I have spent seeing all those doctors—I spent about 30,000 deutsche marks."

Ivica then asked him, "And how much did you pay me?" And the man answered: "I have paid you nothing, sir. I only bought your book, but this is a material product. I know that this book has costs; you have to pay for the paper, the ink, taxes, the workers involved. But you do not ask for anything or accept money for what you give to people through your work. I don't know who you are, but after I saw you, I went back to my doctors and was informed that my illness had simply disappeared. They themselves couldn't believe this had happened. Folks, I never believed in prophets, the supernatural or bioenergetics, but this is real."

What can people do? Most only believe in what they see, but know that the spirit cannot be seen.

Many have met someone who says that they have seen a spirit, an angel or the Mother of God telling them things. But be alert, negative energy exists that can do anything to deceive. Its only limitation is that it cannot create a human being.

And this is how Nenad, once a skeptic, became an ardent believer. In Germany, Switzerland and faraway Africa, he has been spreading the message about Ivica; that there is a man in Zagreb, Croatia, who sees everything, knows everything and helps people. But wondrously, he doesn't charge for his services or ask for any compensation. The only thing that one pays for is a book, which one buys only if he or she wishes to. And often when Ivica sees that a person wants a book but cannot afford it, he gives it to them as a gift.

In February 1995, we were on tour in Germany again. We had to schedule dates for an upcoming tour, but simply didn't know which place or time to choose. This was until Nenad appeared again and said that he would like to invite all of us as his guests to visit the Republic of South Africa. He also informed us that word of the miraculous abilities of Ivica now extended here and people wished to meet him. Ivica and I looked at each other, smiled, and scheduled the trip immediately. A visit was planned from April 16 through May 5, 1995.

Ivica, Dinko, Damir and I left Zagreb together. In Germany, Pajo, Nada and Zora waited for us. The seven of us headed to Johannesburg together. After a 10-hour flight, we landed at the airport, where Nenad, his wife, Ankica, and their daughter, son-in-law and small granddaughter Anna Marija waited for us.

After we refreshed ourselves with some juice and coffee, we headed to their family house that was about 50 minutes away from the airport. Here we were received cordially. There were some tables covered with beautiful tablecloths along the green lawn. On these tables were baskets filled with all possible kinds of tropical fruits: pineapples, mangoes, avocados, bananas and many other kinds that I didn't recognize. Everything had an extraordinary color and everything smelled marvelous, with different kinds of meat prepared in a special way. We all felt very comfortable. We didn't feel tired at all, even though we had spent more than 30 hours traveling.

After some time, the first people who were in need of help started arriving. This was the first time that Ivica had traveled without his mirror, because he thought he was going to rest, not work. In fact, it was the first time in his life that he had wanted to go on vacation. Yet knowing Ivica, I knew that he wouldn't withhold his help. Indeed, soon after the people showed up, he started working. We were all surprised because we asked ourselves: *God, how is he going to work without his mirror?* But this wasn't necessary to ask him, as it didn't bother him and he started predicting their future without the mirror.

The people were surprised by the powers and skills Ivica possessed. He not only told them what he saw, but he also successfully removed their problems. That was something normal to me, nothing strange, for I knew very well who he was and what he was capable of doing. But more about this subject another time. After everyone had been seen, we made our way to the arranged hotel to sleep. Already the next morning, we wanted to go to the sea, heading toward Durban, on the southeast coast of the Republic of South Africa.

At dawn we rented two cars before leaving, a Toyota and a Honda. Nenad drove his own car. This means we left with the twelve of us in three cars. About 50 kilometers before we arrived in Durban, night fell. Since it was fall in South Africa during that time, night was falling at 4 p.m. It was about 27 degrees Celsius (80.6 degrees Fahrenheit).

We decided to go to the nearest hotel on the coast and originally planned to book rooms for only a couple of days, and then continue heading south. But Ivica said, "Braco, book the hotel room for the entire 13 days." That was very surprising for me, for I knew that Ivica didn't like to stay very long in one place. After a night's rest, we tried to figure out the next morning during breakfast how to pass the time in South Africa. I realized that our South African guests, including Zora, Nada and Paja, were expecting to be relaxing at the hotel, for it included a swimming pool and a beach for its guests.

I would have liked the same, but I knew that this wouldn't be the case. Mr. Prokic was a man who not only couldn't stay long at the same place—but he

7

also liked to explore and encounter everything that was new. The black people of Africa delighted him, and each time he saw them, he would honk and wave at them. He liked them in the same way I did, because they were natural and simple people, who didn't crave or long for money. They lived from one day to the next, and we would always see them smiling and happy. Despite the fact that they don't have much of anything, they are richer than we Caucasians are because they have spirit, they have faith; whereas we, unfortunately, do not. We only focus on having more, and the more we have, the more we become stingy. People don't know that when this happens they become their own slaves, because once they have something, they have to be alert that nobody will take it from them. Then they open bank accounts and they fear, God forbid, that there might be a monetary devaluation. People forget that money is only a piece of paper, actually only a number of digits on their account.

We have distanced ourselves from God, and become perpetually tense and nervous. The African people don't have much, and yet, we white people are diverting them from their customs and traditions. We are trying to make them give up their way of life. But who has given us the right to do so? We have come to their lands—and not them to ours. For the same work, an African is paid much less than a white person, even though the result of the work is the same. This is only because of skin color.

Skin color is not a fault, and this is the point.

But people don't realize that they may be white in this lifetime, but in their next life, they could be born as that African, whom the white people oppress and humiliate. Think about this.

After breakfast we went down to the cars and continued to our destination. Ivica said that we were to go toward the mountains. After an agreeable trip of some three hundred kilometers, we found a beach and decided to refresh ourselves in the sea. Ivica began to take off his gold jewelry. I watched him with surprise and when he took off the necklace with the Sun, the symbol that the majority of us wear, I asked him why. He didn't answer, but took all of it off. You can imagine how strange this was for us to watch, for I had never seen him without his gold jewelry. And I asked, "And now what?" He told me to take off my jewelry as well. With displeasure, I agreed. I took all of mine off, except for the necklace with the Sun symbol. And then he said: "Take that off as well." I answered that I didn't want to do it, but he insisted. So I took the necklace off, gave my things to Zora and ran off into the ocean.

My reaction apparently surprised him, for he called Damir and Dinko, and all three of them rushed after me. I went into the ocean, tried to swim, but could not. The waves were high and strong, and they threw me immediately back to the beach. I tried a number of times without success. Then Nenad came over and explained to me that it was practically impossible to swim in the ocean, and for this reason, each house and hotel on the coast of

South Africa had its own swimming pool. Later on, the three of us tried to swim one more time, but now it looked more like splashing in the shallows than swimming.

All of a sudden, Ivica called Dinko and me, and said that he had just had a strange vision in the ocean. He told us how he saw an electrical conductor, which seemed to be located in the ocean and surrounded by three big black holes. Shortly after, he said that Saint Peter appeared to him, giving him the keys to paradise.

After about two hours, we returned to the hotel. Ivica asked me to go to the hotel pool with him. I was taken aback, because Ivica actually didn't like to swim and we had just returned from the beach. I wasn't really up to it, but out of great love for him, I went. After a few minutes, he asked me, "Braco, what do you think, in what way will we work at Srebrnjak 1 after our return from Africa?" I replied, "It will be the same as it is now." He smiled and said: "None of that! I am not some old fortune-teller who predicts the future. That will no longer exist."

"What will happen with the mirror?" I asked, wanting to know. He said that the mirror was very weak for whatever was still to come, and its use was only an intermediary phase. Whatever he meant to say here, you must figure out for yourself.

During dinner, we agreed to return again the next day to the same beach to swim, but it surprised us that Ivica wanted to do this since he hardly ever returned twice to the same place. Around 10:30 a.m.

the next day, we arrived at our destination. The third car was behind us and hadn't arrived yet, so we began to prepare lunch before going swimming.

After lighting a candle, Ivica suddenly said: "Dinko, watch the candle so it doesn't go out. Damir, you call us when the third car arrives, Braco and I are going to swim." I had not heard any of this because I was putting on my swim shorts. When I returned, I saw that Ivica had taken off all his gold jewelry and had thrown it on a seat in the car. I quickly began taking off my jewelry as well, except for the little ring that I wore on the small finger of my right hand—one I still wear today.

I started running after him toward the water. Once again, he looked very strange to me without all of his jewelry. It happened that only the two of us were swimming before lunch. When I reached the water, Ivica was already in up to his knees. I went into the water as well, and when I reached him, something incredible happened. As if carried by an invisible force, we were moved 50 meters into the open sea.

Read very carefully: We weren't swimming, and we weren't carried away by the waves or the ocean current. It was as if an invisible energy moved us. In that moment, we were only separated by a couple of meters, and we tried to get closer to each other, but there was something that was separating us more and more. Then, I instinctively looked back to the open sea and saw a wave many meters high, which was coming toward me. I couldn't do anything and I only thought, *Oh my God, now it's over.*

This gigantic wave buried me under the water and began spinning me around through the turbulence. The ocean had absorbed me like a vacuum. I was rotating rapidly under the surface. I held my breath as long I could, but the moment came when I had to let go, and I simply don't remember anything else.

When I opened my eyes, I saw the sun and could feel the ground under me. I was lying in the water up to my elbows. Without thinking, I got up and headed toward the open sea to start looking for Ivica. I couldn't see him anywhere. I tried to swim without success, as the waves threw me back to the beach. Distraught and weak, I ran to look for help. I yelled: "Damir, Dinko... quickly... I don't' know where Ivica is!"

Everyone came running, and we set out to search for him on the coast. After about three to four minutes, Dinko saw him first. He was floating on the surface of the water with his face down, but we quickly lost sight of him because of the big waves. Then Nenad saw him again, and it was as if a wave simply threw Ivica toward him.

In that moment we all gathered together to help. We dragged him to the beach. We immediately called for help, and while we were waiting for it to arrive, we tried to do everything that was possible to resuscitate him, but all without success. He didn't show any signs of life. A doctor came relatively quickly and confirmed that he had already died in the water.

We all cried like children. We weren't able to believe that the impossible had happened. Everyone except our Ivica could die. A second, a third and finally a fourth doctor came. They all came to the same conclusion: Death had occurred in the water. They told us that we were lucky to have found him, for in the majority of cases, the drowned are usually never found in this ocean. We held on to him for a couple of hours. When the police came, they separated us from him by force.

I wanted to kill myself; I wanted to take my life, and the way did not matter. What did I have a life for without him? I shouted: "No, this is not true, this was not written in his books. He has to come back to life. How can he die?"

Zora came toward me and said: "No, Braco, you mustn't. This is a negative force pushing you. You can't take your own life, because you didn't create it yourself. You will go straight to hell, to the underground world." But I was furious and chaotic inside.

She continued: "If you had to die, you would have drowned with him. You have spent the most time with him, and you know the key. You have to continue. You have to take care of his family: Mara, Alen, Marijana, Karl and Jelka. You have to convey the truth."

I said: "Oh, God. Why did you do this to me? Why didn't you take me as well? What am I going to do all alone?"

2

WHO WAS MR. PROKIC?

Ivica was a man with otherworldly abilities, which science cannot explain. He was a man who could see the past, the present and the future. Not only could he see the destiny of people, but he could also ease their future. In a miraculous way he would solve different kinds of problems. He achieved his greatest success in relationships between men and women. He would bring husbands back to their wives, and wives back to their husbands. I know personally that he saved hundreds and hundreds of marriages.

He was able to remove black magic. I know most of you don't understand this statement. What black magic at the end of the 20th century? Yes, dear readers, this force exists and works like never before. But people don't believe in it, and don't believe that people exist who can cause harm to others, just by using a person's photograph. Such individuals can separate you from your partner, affect your fertility, make your business unsuccessful, cause madness and much more. Only special people who are in contact with the negative energies of the underground world can do this. They are connected through mediumship to it. Everyday life does not draw us to think much about these things. Most of us are not aware that someone can put something in a cup of coffee, juice or any other drink, which can cause mental illness, loss of hair or loss of energy—or which can simply endanger your marriage. Yet, unfortunately, these kinds of things still exist nowadays.

Ivica was one of the few who could oppose this kind of negative energy and remove black magic. Most importantly, he was very successful at it. He dedicated his whole life to people, solved and helped deal with such difficult cases as cancer, blindness, paralysis and different kinds of allergies. No one knew exactly in what way he was doing this all. He simply took all your illnesses and troubles over, and fought against them. In most of the cases, he was successful.

Only if the problem was related to karma from a past life, he wouldn't do anything and would then tell the person involved, "Leave, I am not able to help you." People would leave without knowing why he wasn't able to offer help. But you see, karma means sacrifice. In this situation, people have to accept their lot, and there is no mediating help. God has set a seal on them, which means: Do not intervene. If you see a blind person, you must understand that there is a reason for this circumstance. For example, this could mean that the spirit of this person in a past life was in a military leader who commanded the killing of thousands and thousands of people some hundreds of years ago. That's the reason why this same person was born blind, in order to pay for all the suffering he caused to other innocent souls.

I hope you understand me. For all the sins we commit today, we, as well as our family, will suffer for them now, and will have to pay for them in a future lifetime.

It can occur that you lose a daughter or son, who means everything to you, in an unfortunate accident. In that moment, you would give anything that you have to change things, but in the majority of cases with such karma there is nothing that can be of help.

Our Ivica was actually a person who wanted to be as normal as others, but couldn't be. Why, because this possibility was not in his destiny. The only way that you could tell him apart from other people was his gold jewelry. Believe me, he didn't want to wear it, but he had to. It protected him, and with its help, he was able to help others. This is because energy was flowing through his hands, through the gold, which was destroying the evil around people. Gold gave him strength and it increased his strength at the same time. More gold also became necessary, as his power grew stronger.

You cannot imagine how difficult it was for him during the summers when the temperatures reached over 30 degrees Celsius (86 degrees Fahrenheit). Believe me, it wasn't comfortable for him. In the beginning I thought it easy, but now I can feel it on my own flesh, God forbid. To wear a single ring, one bracelet and a necklace is unproblematic, but more than this is a misery. Yet what can we do, this is our destiny.

In terms of Ivica's private life, he practically didn't have one. He spent the least amount of time with his family—almost never. He was always with people, and the most of the rest of the time he was with me. Some of you might already know that we were always together day and night. Now that he is not among us anymore, I remember every single moment: as if he was here with me, as if he was following me and floating above me. I know that he left me, but I don't know why. Why didn't I go with him? Apparently, it is because I have not completed my karma in my physical body. My candle is still lit, which means that my destiny is still open. What will happen to me remains to be seen.

Ivica loved driving in fast cars; this was something that made him happy. He said that at high speed, he felt as if he could free himself from negative energy and be charged with positive energy. He would drive tirelessly for hours and hours. He especially liked driving at night. During these trips, we would talk uninterruptedly.

I never understood why he dedicated all his free

time to me. Often I felt like an idiot, because I did not understand the majority of the things that he explained to me. I thought, *Oh, my God, he, a great prophet, is wasting time on me.* He would simply reply: "I do what is asked from me. I am with you because I have to be. My child, you still don't understand that, but one day, you will."

And unfortunately, that day arrived where I'm left reflecting. But all of this works in an unusual way. It cannot be understood or learned through teaching. One simply has to possess it, in other words, receive it. Ivica tried to indicate all the various traps life offers us, and there are thousands of them. Each day brings new experiences. The wheel of life is turning in a circle. Our actions are subject to valuation. We go forward at times, and respectively backwards.

All that Ivica created, in the material as well as the spiritual world, he left to us as a legacy. Here in the material he left Srebrnjak 1, for our families, the Community and for us. He also left a spiritual inheritance inside all of us, which helps us feel better.

Many have asked where he acquired all the gold jewelry that he wore. His followers are the ones who gave it to him. It belongs to all of you. He didn't get it drinking, gambling or by selling it. It is still here after his physical death. He only enjoyed this fruit of his work, and acquired it through hard work. I say enjoyed, because he did not do away with any of it, and now other people can continue enjoying his gold jewelry.

It made him especially happy to share with other people. He would share everything he had, even what his followers brought to Srebrnjak 1. People would give him flowers, and these were kept at Srebrnjak 1 or at his house. Once a week, he also sent them to my house. A question people ask is why he loved flowers so much. It was because he was healing us through the flowers. In what way? This I will explain in the future; now it is still too soon.

Probably the majority of people in his place would have sold the various gifts and the flowers that were brought to him, but believe me, he never thought in this way. He was someone who gave money to anyone who needed it. He lent his car, or anything he had, to anyone who asked. He always helped everybody, including his enemies. Very often I asked myself, *God, what kind of a man is this?* I know that many will find it hard to believe, but Ivica had absolutely no interest in business or money.

He hated money, but he needed it in order to publish books, eat, drive cars, visit people's homes and go on tours. So, he had to have it, but he never liked to talk about money. Certainly he had to pay taxes for his company, because if he had not started it, the state would not have given him the authority to perform his services. He spent the smallest amount on himself. He didn't go to casinos, he didn't have any lovers and he didn't spend time in luxurious restaurants. He would rather drive around with me for hours than go to public places.

He was mysterious, for he had a heart stronger than a lion and gentler than a newborn baby. He would easily get mad, but would forgive even faster. I would call him a do-gooder, and everyone took advantage of him.

Often I would tell him, "But Ivica, they are making fun of us." He would smile and say: "Braco, let them, because they don't know what they are doing. Some day, they will understand. May God forgive them until then."

He drank a lot of coffee and smoked cigarettes. In the beginning I thought of cigarettes as harmful to health. But he would say no, for tobacco forces negative energy out of our system. In other words, evil forces flee from smoke. Some Indian tribes nowadays still have the habit of smoking a peace pipe with their friends. Tobacco calms and relaxes the body, works as a kind of stimulus, but not like a drug. Coffee keeps us awake and prevents negative forces from entering our system. Coffee contains a certain ingredient that speeds up the heartbeat and keeps it awake. Yes, he drank a lot of spring water to clean his system, since our physical body is made out of water. This means that Mr. Prokic liked cigarettes, coffee and water. Natural tobacco, coffee beans picked, roasted and brewed without anything else, and mountain spring water just the way God created it. He liked only what Mother Nature had created, without any artificial ingredients and additives.

Ivica also dressed in a down to Earth way and

was most comfortable in his sweatpants or jeans. He didn't like suits or ties. He said that they limited his freedom of movement. He wanted to be ordinary, and most of the time he would make himself less important that the person he spoke to. In equal fashion, he knew how to talk to a farmer, a businessman or an intellectual and he never stood out. He behaved like a regular person. When people forgot that he knew and saw everything, then these same people would try to convince him of something as if they knew better than him. That would be a serious error for these people, for he would immediately start receiving information about them.

He told me: "Look, Braco, people are not good. They will only believe what you say when you help them. But when you allow them to approach you, then they want to know better than you. They think they can learn what I'm doing. They do not understand that it can only be received, because this is a gift that one has to pass on to others. You can't sell it, because you didn't buy it. You don't have any right to do so. Simply, you have to share it with others. But it can't be received by just anyone, only by those who believe and are sincere. Anyone else, believe me, won't receive it. One can't act like God, or imitate him. He created us, and not we him."

This is a common mistake of humanity. Everybody thinks that they can do it all. If you have money, you can buy a car, a house, a plane, lovers or expensive pastimes—but know that love, health and happiness cannot be bought.

Today we are young, but time passes and our candle becomes smaller each second. Each moment, we are getting older and older. Understand that youth cannot be prolonged. Years pass, a new generation comes and then another, and in our old age we say: "Oh God, how quickly my life has passed. What have I suffered for? Whom did I create all this for?"

If you don't have children, then you say: "Oh God, give me children so that I can be a parent." And then, when you have them, after 10 or 15 years, you say, "Oh God, it would have been better not to have them." Because some of these children became criminals, prostitutes or drug addicts, and the parents ask themselves: "Why, God, are my children like this? Why are the neighbor's children different?"

We are not aware that in the majority of cases, we are the ones causing the difficulties for our children. For example: If you have been dishonest toward other people, in whatever manner, it has a direct impact on your family and your children. You thought that nobody could see what was going on. But it is seen. Each moment there are hundreds of departed souls around us, who see and take note of everything, and we are being judged immediately without even knowing it. People don't realize; no one knows this fact.

It can happen that at a certain age we lose our sight or hearing, or suffer from lack of potency or a variety of illnesses. We lose ourselves and we begin to avoid our surroundings, and at the end of our life we don't know what we lived for. We don't even know that it had to be the way it was.

At birth, the same instant a child cries for the first time, his candle of life is being lit on which everything is written down: from birth to death. We don't know how our life is going to unfold. We are not even aware that our previous life is saved there, like on a computer. After taking the information out of our previous lives, a new life is then created. Ivica had access to this information— to our book of life, where he could read this information about us—and would communicate some of it to us.

Obviously he wouldn't tell everything, but only as much as he wanted. What he told you would be your test. If you ever laughed at him, or spoke ill of him, your guardian angel would simply leave and help wouldn't reach you. That's why he always used to tell people, "You are going to get as much help as you believe—no more, no less."

Many supposed that they could buy Ivica's help with money, but this was their mistake. He would send people like this out of his house. He would rather attend poor people than the rich ones. Rich people like this only believed in money; money was God for them. Do you think that Mr. Prokic could have had a lot of money? Yes, he could have. For example, he could have attended a millionaire, whose son was unfortunately suffering from leukemia. This is a common case in reality. A person who has a lot wealth usually has some immediate family suffering from illness.

These people cannot understand that there are evil forces offering them money, but in return it takes the health of their children. It takes all of the children's life forces and sends it directly to the underground world. And at the same time, it gives their parents money. These parents are often too busy thinking of themselves and their fortune, and they don't realize how their children are decaying and that the underworld is absorbing all of their children's energy. When they do realize it, it is already too late. The children are destroyed by then, their energy taken, but their parents, thinking that they can help, go to the most expensive doctors, paying large amounts of money. But in these cases, help is not found.

All the money they have earned, they spend on the health of their children, without knowing that they were the ones who brought this circumstance upon their own children. The children remain sick, and the money, which was gained in an illegal way, disappears the same way it came. The parents devote themselves to alcohol, fights occur and all that has been achieved disappears. This is how these kind of people end up this way.

But don't blame these parents, because perhaps, if you were in their place, you would have done the same. Now, you might say, "No, I wouldn't." Yet, I am sure you might well do the same, because you are not aware of money's capabilities. With it, you feel safe and you think that you can do anything. Indeed, yes, for a certain amount of time you can, as everything goes easily for you. An unseen negative energy gives you the power to have it all. You feel healthy and full of energy. In fact, you are healthy and content with yourself. But don't forget that this evil force wants compensation, and when it wants, it takes energy, such as the health of your children. Initially you don't realize this, but once you do, it's already too late.

Think about it and you will see that from everyone you know, you have witnessed a similar example. But don't forget not to judge anyone, because you don't have the right to do so. Just say, "God, forgive him, for he doesn't know what he is doing."

You are not the judge, and you don't have the right to intervene in the destinies of other people. That can be done only by a few chosen ones. Don't make the mistake and think that you are one of the chosen ones, because that's when you play God. God created us, and we did not create him.

Ivica could have attended to some of these very wealthy people who would have paid anything to have their children cured. He could of made vast amounts of money saving their loved ones, but he never did. Why? To do so would have meant placing a price on the gift he had been given, which he had no right to do. These kinds of people with great amounts of money only believe in something with a price. Since Ivica did not charge a price, they did not think that he knew anything. That's the way people are, thinking that something expensive is worth a lot.

I wish you could now be more aware of how powerful the negative energy is, and how much this evil has snuck into every aspect of human life.

3

THE PATH OF TRUTH

All of you have surely asked yourselves: What was the goal, correspondingly, the path that Ivica traveled? What did he want to achieve?

This path is the path of truth, which he began, and which we continue. This is the path on which we have to prove that he wasn't a black magician or a self-proclaimed prophet, as many called him.

You will see soon who he was. Right now, I can't prove this to you, or maybe some of you would make fun of me. Therefore, I have to remain quiet and wait, and those of you who have listened and read Mr. Prokic's books will understand. I am in an unenviable situation where I am not able to substantiate many things, because I do not have the proof to do so.

Unfortunately, I am not a magician and I can't

do magic tricks. But who knows, maybe something miraculous will happen, maybe you will dream of something or maybe an invisible energy will guide you to Srebrnjak 1.

All of those who come are welcome. I wish those who abandon this path and go another much luck. I don't judge them, for perhaps I would do the same if I were in their place. If later on they change their mind and come back, they are welcome.

I will personally try to follow Mr. Prokic's path just the way he talked about it to me, and our Community follow this goal. How much success we will have, we don't know. It depends on you, for you will judge us. You will expect the same help as before, but now I don't know if you will receive it. I only know that you will come if you receive help, and this is understandable.

Those of us in the Community now—Damir, Dinko, Pero, Ankica, Sara and myself—we don't want to, and won't, imitate or act like Ivica Prokic, because he was unique, and we can only follow him the way he showed us to.

We have to go on, because his books have to be read and reread. He started many things before he left us. If we gave up now, he would remain the person everybody said he was. This means that we have to continue on with the path, the path of truth.

I know that it is going to be difficult and many of you will try to besmirch me. Some of you will think that I am trying to act like and imitate Ivica, and to reap the fruits of his work. But I will do my best to try to withstand everything on this path, because he gave his life for us and I owe him so much.

Right now in this moment, I am entering a living fire, which should swallow me according to all Earthly laws. I don't know how I will escape. Time will tell.

I've always liked excitement and challenges, but this seems almost too much. I will try to help you as much as I can. But, without your belief, I, as well as the other members from the Community, are powerless. If you do not believe, we cannot break through the negative energy that surrounds everyone.

Many wonder if I will look into the mirror and use it. I won't. Mr. Prokic used to predict your destiny using the mirror, and it was a helpful tool. I will not work in the same way he did, because this way has not been given to me. I will work in a new way and how I will do this is not important. You simply need help. So, why care so much about your destiny? What do you need *a prediction* for?

Uncertain, you believe a little bit, but at the same time you don't. I remember the words of our Ivica: "I am not some old fortune-teller who only looks and talks." His goal was completely different than just skimming through the books of people's lives. Perhaps you may have realized, later on, that he disliked doing this, but he did it only because it had to be done this way.

He was very disappointed by people. Often people misinterpreted his words, and these wrong interpretations created a false picture of him. He would say something and people would change the content, and then talk about it with a completely different meaning.

Therefore, it is better that I do not to talk as much, since many of you only believe a little bit. I'm not saying everybody. There are always exceptions, for I am also sure that many do believe. This force coming through Ivica, after it had clearly helped people, convinced many. Would people really still be returning if they hadn't felt anything? No, surely they would not. One would have come once, twice, and then looked for somebody else to help. Many practicing bioenergetics, as well as healers and astrologers, are found in Zagreb, and people compared Mr. Prokic to all of them.

But tell me, who else was able to look into a mirror and perceive a person's past, present and future, while at the same time giving him or her help? No one else could do both of these things. And no one else was able to work with as many people as he did.

If you think it is easy to receive up to 30 people at once, think how tiring it is after only saying "hello" and "good-bye" to everyone. Remember, Ivica worked hard, and there could be no mistakes, no matter how many people came to see him.

People were surprised by the predictions of Ivica, and wondered how he could know these things. He was able to see and to read your book of life. Only a few understand. No, nobody understands.

If Ivica had predicted wrongly, word would have gotten around very quickly. And there wouldn't have been that many people coming every day, nor would there have been invitations for him to go on tours overseas.

Ivica lived to help. Tiredness never overcame him. He created something that was completely unique, and he wrote 13 books, of which some were translated into foreign languages. Unfortunately, he was able to share only a few of them in South Africa. In the future, you will decide if these books will be further available overseas. If you feel they can help, they will be sought after, and if not, they won't be. So, this is the path that we are on now, the path of truth.

But do not think that it will be an easy path for us. Now we will be even more exposed to attacks and cynicism. Remember Ivica's words: "Blessed is the man on whom people spit because of me." Many of you have already destroyed Mr. Prokic's books, because others have told you to do so, and it is as if you have forgotten about the help you received from him.

Do what you have to. If you want to burn a book, burn it. If want to throw it away, throw it away. You can burn all the things that Mr. Prokic gave you. They are yours. But don't forget that you might have problems again. No one forced you to come to Srebrnjak 1. It was your desire.

People swore they would follow Mr. Prokic's

path, but they are not aware that they betrayed him in the same moment that they destroyed, burned or threw away his books. His—and our—books are like seagulls. They have already risen to the heavens, and it is impossible to stop them. The truth is strong and will be recognized eventually.

All the seagulls cannot be destroyed. People can destroy hundreds, even thousands, but not all of them. There will always be someone who will give them shelter. The seagulls are weak now, but soon they will strengthen and rise again to the heavens. Those who are taking care of them now, will be taken care of by them one day. Who knows, maybe there is another bird being born right now, and it will have thousands of young ones. What their future will be like depends on you, because you are the ones who have to protect and take care of them.

4

DOES EVERYONE BELIEVE
IN GOD?

Many scientists, healers and prophets, like each of us, have asked the question: Who is God?

I would say that everyone perceives God in his or her own way. Science does not believe in supernatural phenomena. It tries to demonstrate with various scientific methods and experiments the creation of the Earth, and correspondingly, the creation of man. Nevertheless, many people believe that God is the creator.

Many believe that God is responsible for the creation of the church. So, one should go to church, which is the house of God, and pray there. It is enough to go to church, say a prayer and confess your sins. People believe they will be pardoned and saved this way.

I consider all variations correct. Why not? If people feel this way, and if the church is helping them, then they should just go. Church, as an institution, has existed for more than a thousand years, and there must be something to it, for it has endured from generation to generation. I would tell people to go where they feel good.

Many of us ask ourselves: How was the Earth created? Who created mankind, and how and when? Why do the oceans never dry out? Or, why does the sun never stop shining?

You see, in the beginning of the 21st century, in a time of automation and high technology, people still have not found the answers to such basic questions as how and where it all began. So you will ask yourselves why this is so. It is because people have distanced themselves from nature, respectively from God. Everyone believes in computers, nuclear weapons, thermal power plants and solar energy. We try to create everything artificial, and we distance ourselves more and more from nature.

I know that you will say that you don't have time to go for a walk in nature. There are chores, work, cleaning your apartment or house, etc. But now I'm asking you: How then is it possible that you have time to spend hours and hours in front of the television, staring at the computer, sitting in stuffy or smoke-filled rooms, or gossiping about each other?

One day while watching a television commercial, I saw that man's technology is now so advanced that it's no longer necessary to go to a store to do shopping. It is enough to call a number to order a product, and in a short amount of time the desired item will be at your door.

Meanwhile, the invention of the microwave oven allows food to be prepared in a faster way than it was by our grandmothers. Food that is prepared in this way appears to be appealing, but is it healthy? We don't really know how much of the nutrition of the ingredients is maintained using a microwave. And this is something that television and commercials won't tell us.

You haven't asked yourselves if high temperatures destroy the nutritious ingredients that are essential for our organism. Our children live off of hamburgers, hot dogs, Coca-Cola, sandwiches and pizza. All of this looks fantastic, but what are they made of? We probably don't want to know.

When was the last time you went for a walk when you were simply carefree, without fatigue and without plans? We live in a time where everything is intense, and it is as if everything will simply explode.

It sounds incredible, but I know that many children who live in the city have never seen a horse, a cow or a chicken. But surprisingly, it is more important that this same child knows how to operate a computer, knows something about business and can speak a couple of foreign languages. And when that child is asked to describe the appearance of a pear, a cherry, or a fruit tree, he will just look at you strangely.

Here you have an example of what we humans

believe in. Science is so advanced that we have created weapons that could destroy all of us. It would be enough for some fanatic to push a button for a catastrophe to take place. We have created weapons to protect ourselves. From whom? From ourselves.

We people are worse than animals! We have created weapons, and now we don't know what to do with all these armaments. So we agree to destroy some of them. But then why have we even created any of them?

I would say that evolution is progressing slowly, for a true human being has not been created yet. We have distanced ourselves from God—and from nature—and we don't even have time to think about nature, let alone enjoy it.

When was the last time you went for a walk through a park or forest and listened to the chirping of the birds? Or tried to count how many different bird songs you hear at the same time, while touching the grass, plants or a flower with your hand? Or even leaned on a tree trunk?

Try it, for that's when you will make direct contact with nature. You are not even aware that in these kinds of moments, your organism is receiving and being charged with energy directly from nature, from God.

Understand that you also come from nature, and allow your body to be in physical contact with it at least sometimes. Observe and walk on green lawns and forests, breathing deeply, because your body is eager to get some fresh air.

And now my dear readers, I will try to explain how I am experiencing God and Mother God respectively. For me, God is the light. The sun is the crown of everything.

I know that you don't understand this at all, but slowly you will understand. The sun is the creator, and in turn, the source of life on Earth. And the Earth is Mother God. When I refer to the Earth, I mean the entire world and not only to the part that you're standing on. The Earth comprises everything—tables, chairs, cars, planes, food—and everything that we can touch comes from the Earth, from Mother God.

The more you think about it, the more you will realize that everything that we have and make is comprised of resources from the Earth. Even our physical body is Earth, consisting of her elements. In the moment that our soul leaves our body, our candle goes out; our body is worthless and becomes only matter, a thing without life. So, every physical thing has its lifetime. The same way this applies to a human body, it applies to an animal's body. The same goes for plants. Each plant has its own lifetime. Even a house, or the apartment that you live in, has written in its destiny how long it will last. It could be 10, 20, 200 or 500 years, but eventually its time will come.

I hope that you understand so we can move on. Let me simplify for you: For me, God is the Sun, respectively the light, and Mother God is the Earth. Therefore, do not say that you have seen Mother

God, that she appeared in a special way to you and told you things. There's nothing to such claims. Mother God is omnipresent. All that we are able to see with our eyes is Mother God, the Earth.

Remember, God never works wonders. God's force cannot be seen; it simply has to be felt. People have forgotten that the negative energy can do everything too, except for creating human life. God loves man, and that's why he has created mankind. But the negative energy hates man, and therefore, is doing everything possible to make people hate God. That's the reason why people are distancing themselves more and more from God, but without even being conscious of it. So now we know, God, the creator of all, is the Sun; and Mother God who gives birth is the Earth. This is how it works.

The Sun, with the help of its rays, fertilizes Mother God, the Earth, and creates life in this way. This means: God, the Sun, creates, and Mother God, the Earth, bears.

You will ask: how does it fertilize? It does it the same way a man fertilizes a woman, with his semen, from which new life is created. The Sun fertilizes Mother Earth: It sends its rays down, and they are the semen that creates new life. This means that the Sun is the key to everything. It constantly watches and protects Mother God. But we humans still don't know the strength and power of the Sun. We are not aware of how dangerous it is. God is very angry with people because they are distancing themselves from him more and more. We all live with the expectation that something is about to happen. We all are waiting for Judgment Day.

The church foresees the end of the world, and that the dead will arise from the grave. Regarding the rising of the dead, this means that the souls of departed people, which are imprisoned, will rise and be the ones to judge—and I agree. The return of Jesus Christ, the Son of God, is told about as well. I would also agree that he will return, but not in physical form the way people think of him. This is an illusion. When he returns, he will come to judge. Two thousand years ago he took away all the sins of this world. The moment he returns, a baptism of fire will start. Up until now, it has been a baptism with water.

Do you understand me now? The Sun will increase its intensity. It will chastise people because they don't believe in God. Great droughts will come; rivers and lakes will dry out. Volcanoes will be activated anew, causing a great pollution of the air, and people will start disappearing.

Droughts will happen immediately when this begins. Those who have their spiritual guides free will be saved, because with the help of their intuition, they will be kept from harm. For the rest who now grab, rob and kill; there will be no salvation.

After the great Judgment Day, happiness, love and well-being will reign. After that, Atlantis, the long lost continent, the sister of Mother God, which God saved and isolated to a safe place, will appear.

The sea will reveal its secrets, which are still being hidden. Nobody knows yet what the depths of the sea possess. The North as well as the South Pole will speak for themselves, for the Earth still has surprises, which are unknown to man. You ask yourselves: How is it possible that people have not yet discovered these things?

Understand that in comparison to God, humanity is still nothing. It can only go as far as God permits. But now the end of everything is coming. The truth must be known. Each one will be judged for his actions. At the time of birth, God puts a seal on each of us, by which each of us is distinguished and our life followed. In the same moment a mother hears the first cry of her newborn child, the spirit enters the body. His candle is being lit in the heavens, and that's how his life begins.

Understand that the body is nothing without the spirit. So who speaks through our mouths? Well, I will tell you, sometimes it is the souls of people who have died a long time ago. They simply enter our body and talk, as though they are us. How often does one say something without even being aware of it? We have all noticed how someone can change markedly a couple of times during the same day. It depends on how many times that person is being visited by a different spirit. This is why sometimes you feel happy, sometimes sad, sometimes tired and sometimes full of energy. In this way, Mr. Prokic tried to neutralize the negative energy that came through us, and exchanged it for positive instead. It sounds better this way, doesn't it?

The path that I follow is the path that our Ivica started. He was the foundation, the first link of the chain, to which all else is added. We are the next links that follow, who must read about him and respectively spread the truth, for truth is the best and strongest weapon. God tracks and notes everything carefully, and therefore do not think that he will abandon you. When we think that there is no salvation for us, that we have reached the end of our strength, something miraculous will happen and we will be saved. Well, now you ask yourselves what to believe in. Today, everyone believes in the power of money. Let's agree that we can't survive without money. So this being true, we must preside over money, and not allow it to be the master of us. Because people created money—it did not create us.

I know that this time of crisis that we're living in will be over one day, for after every rainstorm, the sun comes out. But we all must understand that people are to blame for everything, and they must pay for it now. People are in a bad temper, they seem to be repulsed by each other, and in their arrogance, they don't even know what to do with themselves. This is happening all over the world. Why?

Because the time of cleansing is approaching when only the chosen ones will be saved. For this reason: Love each other, don't hate, and love your enemy the way you love yourself.

Ivica taught us to first help others, and then ourselves. And even if you see that others are making fun of you, let them do so and say, "Oh God, forgive them, for they do not know what they are doing." The truth is that those people in such moments are under the greatest influence of negative energy, respectively the underworld, without being aware of it. Don't ever judge anyone, because that's when you play God, and you do not have any right to do so. Leave judgment for those to whom the right to judge has been given.

Let's try to live and end this life with dignity, so that our progeny will not have to be ashamed, but instead can be proud of us. For when they mature, when they grow up, our candle will be extinguished. That's when we, our spirits, will help them the same way our ancestors, our deceased loved ones, are helping us. And now, at the end of this chapter, let's ask ourselves if we indeed believe in God, for God is everywhere around us and wherever we wish him to be.

It is not enough to just believe when we are going through bad times; on the contrary, we should pray and thank our creator when we are also doing well. That's when we will find that our negative energy—the negative souls of the deceased ones which surround us and that enter our bodies—simply leaves. God is the light; he is everywhere around us, and each little piece of gold that we own, be it a ring, a necklace or a bracelet, should be honored. Through gold, God accompanies and helps us. Nevertheless, one day these bad times will be over, and peace, love and well-being will reign.

5

WHY DOES MAN EXIST?

I am sure that there is no one in this world who has not asked the following question at least once: "Oh God, why was I born and what is the purpose of my life? Everything that I have created will one day be destroyed."

Yes, in the majority of circumstances, this is the case. There are those who build and those who destroy. Man is an Earthly being and he has to exist, just like the animals and plants, like the water, like the city or village, like all of creation. Everything is connected, and one thing cannot exist without the other. Neither can people exist without the animals, nor the animals without people.

How? In this way: Man needs animals for food, for making shoes, for making clothes, for recreation and companionship. On the other hand, these animals need man. People have to provide them with a home, food and warmth, and give them love, which the animals will return to the people when they least expect it. At times when you think that the world has collapsed and that everyone has abandoned you, the animals you care for will always welcome you, will somehow cheer you up and give you back the faith in life improving, in a better tomorrow. Unlike people, a dog or cat will never betray you.

It's the same with plants. We cannot exist without them, for they produce oxygen, without which life is simply not possible. But the way people are now, they cut down and destroy the forests without considering that this vital mantle around our globe is becoming smaller and smaller, and the ozone holes bigger and bigger. They don't think about future generations and the quality of the air they will have to breathe.

So, everything is a part of an interdependent chain: people, animals and plants.

Yes, there is the water, which also contains life, but the underwater world is ruled by different laws of life than the Earth. God also created flora and fauna in rivers, lakes and seas. But the animals, fish and plants are accustomed to a different lifestyle in this environment. Men, as they are, continue to attempt to penetrate the underwater world, but they are not successful because the time has not yet come. God obviously is still not permitting humanity to see what kinds of secrets the depths of the oceans are hiding.

Therefore, man exists so that the entire chain can function. If we take away any of the links, we will see that life on Earth would not be possible. But people think that they are more important and that life is possible without everything, except them. They are not aware that everything is predetermined and written in the heavens, and this means how and in what way they will live.

Each time period and each civilization brings this predetermined circumstance of conditions with it. After some time, one dies out and a new one is created. Thousands of years ago, people lived in a different manner than today. They didn't fly in airplanes, drive cars or sleep in luxurious houses and hotels. Back then, people were devoted and faithful to nature—and to God. They didn't visit the doctor all the time. In our neighborhoods, we can see nursing homes, pharmacies and hospitals everywhere around us. Ask your grandmothers or great-grandmothers, many of them never consulted a doctor or dentist during their lives. Whereas nowadays, children often have bad teeth before entering elementary school, as much has developed for the worse. We are destroying ourselves, even if we don't want to accept it. Now people are inventing everything possible to have more time left over. Then they bestow their so-called free time directly to the underworld.

That's why wars, diseases and droughts come. God is watching and noting this all, without interfering in man's desires. Therefore, how much longer people will keep living like this depends on them.

Obviously we are still not aware that we are sleeping, that our spiritual guide is asleep. This is because we exclusively act based on how we perceive things in our physical environment, but we don't listen to our inner *self*, to our intuition. We don't listen because we don't understand that this is how we close ourselves down, and are thus left exposed and unprotected to the influences of the material world. We don't allow our organism to throw out the negative energy. Lacking this help, the only thing we know to do is to shout at each other, most of the time without any reason. Often we behave in this way as if we were hypnotized, and we remain unaware of our behavior until someone brings it to our attention.

When we act in this way, we are being misguided by the influence of the negative energy through a bad spirit, and this negative spirit is a deceased person who enters into us. At such times, we simply are unaware of the words that we are saying and our behavior. This means that our body is like a filter through which energy flows ceaselessly. The fact is that people don't recognize when this energy is positive and when it is negative. When we are nervous and tense, when everything is getting on our nerves for no reason, that's when negative energy flows through our bodies. Or, to make it simple: The negative spirit of a departed person, which is creating a bad influence, has entered our bodies and is trying to mislead us, fuel fights, extend hate or seduce others through us. We are in a form of trance, and not aware that we are used in such moments by the underworld, and that we will continue to feel like this as long as the negative spirit is in us. How long this state will endure depends on us. However, ordinary people don't know this.

Usually we recognize negative and destructive behavior in other people, but not so easily in ourselves. Here we often have blinders, thinking ourselves perfect, and that everybody else can transgress except us.

I think that you are now asking yourselves about what to do in this situation. How can we help these people, in order to help ourselves?

First, do not get into a fight with these people, for that's the underworld's goal. As soon as you are provoked, lose your temper and start fighting back, this evil force has succeeded in making you lose control of yourself. Then you fall under the influence of the negative energy, and this same negative energy jumps into you—better said, the bad spirit controlling that individual shifts into you. And that is how the negative energy spreads from one person to another. The best thing to do is to stay calm and respond with love.

You may ask me: How do I respond with love when someone is insulting me, wishing me ill and hating me? Well, if you really love that person sincerely, from your heart, you will then help that person in that moment. A negative spirit will leave in the face of love, disarmed by it, and that person's natural happiness, love and well-being will return again. Do not ever blame or judge a person in this situation, because you could find yourself under a similar influence tomorrow.

The same moment that the negative energy feels love, it flees. As soon as the negative spirit has left, the person under its influence feels better, carefree and as if nothing has happened, often being oblivious of his or her own words and behavior earlier.

So, whenever somebody is in trouble, the point is to help and not to criticize, for that's how a counterproductive effect is achieved. The remedy is simple: love—but this is a virtue that few possess. It's just how people are at this time, not wanting to do something the simple way if it can be made complicated.

It seems that nowadays the goal is to be more complicated than one is, without even knowing the reason why. Why do people even desire such a thing? They probably think that this makes them more interesting in society and gets them more attention, but they are oblivious to how lost they look.

Nevertheless, people are still sleeping and will keep sleeping until the point comes when they realize that they have to go back to nature, for everything starts and ends there. When we go back to nature and realize that it created us, and not the other way around, we will then look at a lot of things differently and more simply. But until then we will keep spinning in the spellbound circle.

Who is to blame? We ourselves chose this way so far. Isn't it so?

6

BRACO'S ARRIVAL AT
SREBRNJAK 1

So the time has come for me to tell you something about myself, and how I came to Srebrnjak 1.

I was born on November 23, 1967, in Zagreb, Croatia, at 6:15 a.m. I graduated from the College of Commerce in Zagreb, and then I went on to further study at the University of Commerce and graduated after four years. Next, I pursued postgraduate studies, obtaining my master's degree in Economic Sciences at the age of 24.

I know all of you will ask yourselves what this has to do with my current lifestyle. I will tell you that it has nothing to do with it. Nevertheless, I had to complete this phase of my life, and afterwards, I immediately founded my own private company with the help of my father. He passed on his knowledge of business with much love and hope for my future, step-by-step to me.

Honestly, I lived a perfect life. I had everything anyone could wish for, in the material sense. I drove fast and luxurious cars, such as Mercedes, Audis and Porsches. I went out to the most exclusive places and discos, and was dating all the girls that I wanted. It sounds perfect, doesn't it? Like in a fairy-tale.

However, all of this seemed empty and too easy. I was an oddity in this environment, living in my own world, and I loved exciting situations and risks. I didn't like the jet set of rich people or the places they would go, even though I used to go out with them. Over time, it all began to disgust me. I experienced situations in which people only paid attention to what kind of clothes and shoes you wore, what kind of car you drove and how much money you had in your pocket. One had to have a certain kind of "pedigree" in order to be part of their society, and after a short amount of time, it became monotonous and boring to me.

Yet, I had to get to know and experience this "lifestyle" before coming to Srebrnjak 1. Why? If I hadn't gone through it all, I surely would have become conceited and eventually ended up seduced by this way of life. But I went through all of this before the age of 26, so I had these experiences, eliminating the desire for them later on. It all had value, and this is why the kind of stratum a person belongs to is immediately recognizable to me.

I went through many experiences until my

arrival at Srebrnjak 1, so that nothing would draw my attention away once reached there. You cannot buy me with money, because it simply doesn't mean anything to me. For me, it is only something that drives people to do bad things to each other, even to kill. I know that we cannot live without money, but we have to become the master of it, and not the other way around—falling under its influence. In most cases, the latter occurs more often.

As soon as people accumulate a lot of money, they begin to change; they feel somehow more secure and think that no one can harm them. I am telling you this because of my own experience. Understand that money is temporary. It goes the way it comes. If nothing else, it will be spent by your children when you least expect it. Therefore, do not fear it, and don't desire more and more. Try to live normally, in the same way as when you didn't have money, for that's when you will be the master.

Now, you're asking me what happens with those who live with an income that is insufficient for utilities, bread and milk, and who lead a day-to-day existence. It is true there are many such people. They are in such a phase and have to overcome it. Maybe one day the Sun will shine on them as well.

Some people indeed don't have money, but their hearts are full and their souls gentle. They will always console and tell you some kind word when you are going through bad times, which will mean a lot to you. Observe them and you will realize that they are somehow calmer and happier even though they don't have much. Their guardian angel protects them, and something good always happens that delivers aid to them during the most difficult times. Meaning, God will never abandon them.

When I look at today's youth, I realize how rapidly they are changing. They are surrounded by drugs, alcohol and money—and nothing else. Fast food, hot dogs, hamburgers and pizza are their exclusive diet, and then when they get sick, we ask what from. Look at our young people: They sleep the whole day; they don't do anything, but are always tired. Why?

Because the underworld is taking their energy, and in return it offers them discos, bars, drugs and alcohol. Young people do not know that as they pass the night in these dark spaces filled with alcohol, drugs and loud, abrasive music, the negative energy is able to enter them. And their spiritual guide is blocked, namely asleep. So they sink, their energy taken, until they are finally immersed. Let's not blame them, because they are not aware of what is taking place. This happens quickly.

The negative energy is always standing in the wings throughout the course of life. In elementary school, your child is an excellent student, well-behaved, friendly, a sweet child and a real angel. So, you boast about your child everywhere possible, unaware that there are people who don't like this because they are jealous of your situation and happiness. Hiding their jealousy, they pretend to be your best friend, but are working to ruin your angel—your child.

You will ask how this is possible, but it is so. Such people's negative effects on your child will extinguish him, little by little, and you won't even know this is happening. By the time your child enters high school, you begin to notice that he is progressively changing. He begins to withdraw, wanting to be alone, as you, his parent, get on his nerves. He begins to shout that nobody understands him. If you ask him something or if you try to show him the right way, he considers you his biggest enemy.

But that is only the beginning. You then step back and try to talk to your spouse about the situation, decide to go to your child's school and find total chaos there. You don't recognize your child anymore. There are no more outstanding grades, and instead a lot of unexcused absences. Your child has not only become a problem for the teachers, but also for the other students. Right here is when parents lose control over their child and themselves. Since they can't calm their child, parents think the only possibility left is to take him to the doctor.

These kinds of cases usually end up at the psychiatrist, where the doctor gives the child medication that contains stimulants, which at first calms him. Most parents are unaware that the child's body is progressively getting used to these medications, and once it becomes accustomed to them, his body can't function without them. I am talking exclusively about medicine that affects the psyche, specifically its capacity for calmness—not about every kind of medicine, but exclusively about this group. This is how, after some time, a child becomes addicted to them.

We all know that our body consists of millions of cells, and the way those medications calm our body is by destroying the harmful ones; but also, at the same time, side effects occur that destroy positive cells. Every medicine works in a positive and negative way in the organism. It is not my intention to say anything against medicine. Only that it is necessary to prevent the causes of our ailments. But when it comes to a disease, it is usually already too late to act. Here, God has also created medicine, and one must respect it.

The same goes for doctors, which God has created because they live as part of the chain of life. Apparently we cannot live without them. We, therefore, have to respect and appreciate them like every other profession. Understand that it is not easy to become a doctor nowadays. It is necessary to spend more than a decade studying before engaging to fight for someone's life, any patient's life. They have decided to dedicate this earthly life given them, and all of the knowledge they attained from their previous lives, to others. Therefore, their destiny is to heal people. Each profession is a link in the chain without which we cannot live.

And now I will describe how I came to Srebrnjak 1. On the August 10, 1993, around 2 p.m., I was watching tennis with my father in our home. My mother was hurriedly getting ready to go somewhere. I asked her where she was going, and she said that she didn't have time for an explanation and would tell me later when she returned. My father and I only looked at each other; we shrugged our shoulders and thought, *typical woman.*

Approximately an hour later she came back, breathless, and asked me for a small photo of myself. Confused, I asked her what she needed it for. She told me that in Zagreb, on Srebrnjak Street, there was a man who saw and knew all. All you had to do was show him the picture of the person you were interested in. I thought that my mother was foolish because she went to see such idiots. I told her that such people were charlatans. I didn't believe in any of it, as until that moment I hadn't been to see any of these kinds of people. Nevertheless, I gave her my picture. My father and I exchanged a look again and thought, *senseless woman, what does she know.*

Around 6 p.m., my mother returned. Upon entering the room, she told me that the man she had gone to see was named Ivica Prokic, and that he knew all and had told her everything about me. I asked her: "What could he possibly know about me?" My thought was *nothing at all.*

I realized that she was carrying a yellow book in her hands, and I asked her what it was. She told me that it was a book written by him, which he had dedicated to her with his signature of hieroglyphs, and that one would feel better just by reading it.

At that point I was really worried about my

mother's health. I thought that she had gone crazy. I said aloud, "Oh God, why did this have to happen to my mother?" She got a little bit angry, left the book on the table and said: "You don't believe in it, that's fine. But if you want, you can read the book." I laughed and said to her, "As if I don't have anything better to do than read some idiot's book."

Nevertheless, out of curiosity, I took the book in my hands, and when I flipped through it and saw his photo, and I thought: *Oh, my God, what kind of gypsy did she go to? Who does he think he is wearing all that gold?*

Without thinking, I put the book down and began reading the newspaper. But after a few minutes something awakened inside of me, and I took the book in my hands and started skimming through it again.

After having read the first page, I wanted to ask my mother to tell me something more about him, but I quickly remembered that I had just criticized him a few moments ago. You can imagine how I felt. God forbid this happens to anyone. I wanted to know more about him, but how? The only one who was able to tell me more was my mother. She, as mothers often do, immediately realized that I was sorry. She approached me and said, "Read the book, and later, if you want, we can go to see him together." She hadn't even finished the sentence, and I found myself in my room, reading the book, literally swallowing the words. I read it in one breath.

Afterwards I went to my mother and asked, like a child, when we were going to see him? She said that we would go on Monday, October 11. I realized that I still had to wait an entire week, but I was happy to have the honor to get to meet him. On October 11, 1993, I arrived at Srebrnjak 1 at 9 a.m. with my mother. I was first surprised, then curious, about how my first meeting with this man was going to go. I felt excitement and some strangely pleasant energy flowing through my body. The same as you are feeling now while reading this book. He was sitting, smoking a cigarette and drinking coffee. Our eyes met and I immediately felt that Mr. Prokic distinguished himself from the others.

That was enough for me to decide to wait and see what was going to happen next. My mother approached him and, without hesitating, asked him if he could come to her home and sanctify it. He only smiled and asked, "Mrs., how many times have you been here to Srebrnjak 1?" She said that she had been there only once. He said that she was crazy and that it was usually necessary to wait some years before he went to his followers' homes. This didn't disconcert her; she only said that her son had come with her.

That was when Mr. Prokic looked at me, rose from his chair and walked toward me. "What do you need, young man?" he asked me. I responded that I had read his book and that an energy had suddenly brought me there.

He then said abruptly: "Wait for your turn, but

keep in mind that sometimes you have to wait for hours. And you, lady, go home." My mother turned away and left. He seemed somehow wild, yet I felt that he was natural, as if he didn't pretend in any way, not in front of anyone. Simply, if you like it, come, and if not, good-bye and go. That only reinforced my desire to stay even more.

When the time came, I entered his office with about 30 people. I thought, *How will he able to work with all of us at once?* I didn't have to wait long until he began to work with one person after another. He talked quickly and clearly. I saw that people were taking books and leaving. I only thought, *Hopefully, I am going to be the last person.* The crowd was getting smaller, and in the end, there were only three of us left.

That's when I knew I was indeed going to be the last one. Fear was slowly creeping in, and I said to myself, *Oh no, what am I going to do now?* For indeed, in the room where there were once 30 of us, only he and I were left.

His first words were: "And as you can see, young man, you are the last one left just as you desired. Right?"

I only mumbled something, I don't even know what. I simply wasn't able to speak. He then started telling me some things that had happened in my life so far that no one but me knew about. According to this, I realized that no one could have told him about these things. And this was my first time seeing him.

He told me who I was, what I was, the problems

I had met in life and much more. But I will tell you about this all another time. Now it's still too early. That was when I felt the end had come to my aimless roaming. I felt that I had found at Srebrnjak 1 exactly what I had been seeking all along. Yes, this was that place. A place where people came, regardless of what nationality they belonged to. Here, it was not important if they were old, young, ugly or beautiful. In this place, we were all the same, equal. Profession was not important, neither was social class. We simply were all people and were all created by the same God.

I knew Mr. Prokic as a person with simplicity about him, who was very natural and direct. He would tell you the truth, face-to-face, whether you liked it or not. That's the way he was, and the way people liked him. Even though he was not a common sort of man, he didn't want us to distance ourselves from him at all.

He didn't talk much about his abilities. They were his gift from God, which he had received and gave freely to others without any price. One doesn't have the right to sell what is received as a gift, because you didn't pay for it. I hope you understand me.

He would always repeat that people would receive help to the extent they believed. Not more, and not less. But people didn't understand this. Why, because people don't know what they should believe in. You should believe in yourself, in your feelings. You should believe in love and not hate.

It is important to understand that our body is only matter; this is what we see with our physical eyes. But the body is lifeless, that is nothing, without spirit. It is the spirit that talks through our mouths. Life is created only when spirit and body are connected together. Yet people always think about the body, while ignoring the spirit. We haven't asked ourselves what kind of force it is that speaks through our mouth or influences our life.

I will repeat the answer one more time: It is the spirits of deceased people; these souls enter into us and speak through our mouths. I will not tell you more now, for I have already said too much.

Think a little about all of this and realize that the spirit has to be differentiated from the body. People are still sleeping, and it is time to start waking up. The awakening is just about to begin.

7

WHY DID PEOPLE VISIT IVICA PROKIC?

Some of them would come in curiosity, some out of provocation, and others didn't even know why they had come. The majority, however, came because they were driven by an invisible energy.

So, they came because they found there an inner peace without even being aware of it. Our earthly body is exposed to external stimuli, and this is how we pass through positive and negative energy, without understanding what is taking place. You will ask yourself: how? I will explain.

The human eye is capable of perceiving things in our physical environment, but only the things that are material. If you look through the air, you won't see anything, only emptiness. This is something that nobody has yet successfully deciphered. We people think that this is only empty space through which we move. Yet some of it is positive, and some negative. While we move through space, respectively the air, these energies freely enter and exit our body. I know this sounds incredible to you, but this is the truth, which I cannot prove materially to you. But in time I will, and you will see how it works.

In that moment when negative energy, a bad spirit of someone deceased, enters our body, we feel different kinds of problems, such as an accelerated heartbeat, shortness of breathe, dizziness, sudden sweating, loss of energy, nausea, etc. If you then go to see a doctor, it will often happen that all your tests show that you are well, but meanwhile you feel worse and worse. The doctors will sometimes think that you are a hypochondriac, because everything seems to be all right with you. Then you simply begin losing faith in yourself, in those close to you and in the doctor. Your family members will make fun of you and tell you: "Why are you making this up? Don't you see that your medical tests are all right? You don't have anything."

Don't blame the doctors, for no X-ray or microscope can perceive a deceased soul. This has not been achieved so far. Medicine can only cure what it sees, because this is its God-given territory. Similarly, ordinary people, specifically through the scientific method, cannot investigate God. Access to this has not been granted.

So here is why the majority of people come to Srebrnjak 1. Because here they receive the energy that simply repels the spirit of someone deceased out of their body. And after some time, one feels good, no longer taken over by the negative influence. But this process cannot occur unless you believe. This means that you must be driven by some desire, something has to awaken inside of you, in order for you to come. When your spiritual guide senses danger and leads you to come, that is when you do indeed come, because the spirit senses danger before the body does. Therefore, listen to your spirit and let it guide you. But don't try to convince anyone to come, even if you feel they need too, for they cannot come if it's not destined. That person will feel fear, disgust or will find an excuse not to go. But don't worry; they will come the moment their spiritual guide awakens. Until then nothing will happen.

Just be natural and let your body, by means of your spirit, guide you. That's when you are certain not to make a mistake. When you come, come spontaneously, without any obligations. Don't plan your visit, for when you make a commitment, perhaps you will not be able to fulfill it. Why?

Because something may come up soon after and lead you astray, preventing your plans. Negative energy, specifically the negative spirit of some departed soul, will hear your thoughts. It will immediately throw something in your way that will prevent you from coming: an unexpected job offer that brings you great gain, an invitation to the movies or the theater, or if you are younger, simply going out with your boyfriend or girlfriend.

Understand that the evil force is capable of doing and creating anything, except for creating a human being. That's why it does everything to distance human beings from God. Then you will think, *Well, I will go to Srebrnjak 1 another time.* But we are forgetting that our spiritual guide has already foreshadowed some danger in advance. But here the negative energy has already misled you, capturing your attention away from your right path. We are not aware that we are making a mistake in that moment. After a few days, we begin dealing with problems, insomnia, nightmares, etc. We will then seek help, but the way to salvation will be much longer and painstaking. So, listen to your feelings and let them guide you.

Do not come under the influence of others, for you're not aware of who or when a spirit speaks through them. You cannot determine if it is positive or negative energy, if it is a positive or negative spirit of some deceased person.

Read between the lines. I know that many hands will hold this book, and therefore, I have to be careful about what I say and how I write things. I have to be careful not to hurt anyone. That is not my intention at all.

First of all, I want to show people the way that lies in front of them. They just need to open their eyes.

8

THE AWAKENING

Finally, the time has come for people to understand that they consist of their spirit as much as they consist of their body. And also that God created them—not the other way around.

When God created the earth, the Mother God, he didn't create any borders between countries. People have done this. He didn't create any religions. There was only one belief: the belief in God, in a better tomorrow, the belief in nature.

Nowadays, people have completely changed. People think that they can dominate others. That's the reason why wars occur. In the same way that God created well-being and love, evil created hatred, a living hell. Instead of believing in each other and coming together in unity, people are splitting more and more apart and hating each other.

Instead of borders being eliminated, they are being tightened up and secured. So, we are distancing ourselves from each other, unconscious of the result.

As long as we keep doing and thinking in this way, there will be wars, innumerable disturbances, kidnappings and drugs. Understand that God doesn't want to interfere if people choose to reject him.

You may ask: How are we rejecting God? We are rejecting him by hating each other, because we are not cognizant that God loves people. This is why he is creating us. He loves all people: the white, the black, the yellow, the fat, and the skinny. Appearances are only temptations through which God is testing us.

You may not be aware that in the moment you judge someone and say, "Look at that alcoholic, crazy, killer," that you are insulting God, because God has created everything.

Until we recognize these basic things, we will remain asleep. Not us, but our spirit—our spiritual guide. The moment we start to think in a different way, our spirit will begin waking up more and more, and we will return to nature, correspondingly to God.

Then the day will come when people will realize that we are all equal, that we all come from the same God; the wars will stop, and all weapons will become silent.

Hence, the first part of this book is entitled, *The*

Awakening. It should progressively awaken your spiritual guide, which is sleeping. When it awakens, it will guide you with the help of your intuition. That's when your body will react to danger on its own, and you will be able to recognize what is good and what is bad on your own.

Know that our Ivica will guide and protect us, because he started this all, and we are simply the next link in the chain, with the task to spread love, for love is the most powerful weapon.

Photos

BRACO & IVICA

From 1993 through 1996

Ivica Prokić
1950 - 1995

Part II

THE SUN

9

THE BEGINNING

First of all, I would like to describe everything that has happened since May 5, 1995. All of you should know that this was my first day of working in a special way. I wouldn't like anyone to experience the same situation, God forbid. First of all, I would like to thank all of my closest colleagues, who have stayed with me and have never let me down. But if you think that everyone was supportive, you are mistaken. Some even tried to backstab me after the tragic event while I was still in South Africa. Certain people with a dishonest intent wanted to stop the work, and others tried to persuade my followers to seek help from those who dedicate themselves to astrology instead. I was aware of all of this, but I had to pretend as though I didn't see what was happening around me. Those were my temptations, to see if I would continue the work. People attacked me and tried to get rid of me a couple of times, but thanks to those who came to see me each day, I remained at Srebrnjak 1. May God forgive the person who was near me every day, but still acted behind my back. I do not hate this person, and I have forgiven her. I will punish her with my love, for I don't know any other way.

I know that many think that I have been reaping the fruits of Ivica's work. At times, I have thought about this as well. But understand that I didn't know I would be here in this way, nor was I seeking it. All of you know that Ivica had been permanently near me, in good as well as in bad times. It's better not to tell you everything we've been through. In the last couple of months, everyone has insulted us. After an attack by the press, a lot of people left. Now, a year later, these same people have come back looking for help from me. How do you think I feel in such moments? Regardless of that, I try to help everyone equally. That is the force that keeps us together. Ivica himself called me his right hand and named me in his books. I did not want or know this would be done.

At the same time as you insult me, you are insulting Ivica. I know that many of you would like to be in my place. If you have the desire, come and help yourself. I will cede my place to you, and you can try to do the same work.

If you think that I am here because of money, you are mistaken. Before my arrival at Srebrnjak 1, I had much more than I do now. Money, as a medium of personal enrichment, does not interest me—only as a medium for fulfilling common needs. The gold jewelry that I am wearing is yours—you gave it to Ivica. It was bought with your money. The food that my Community, Mr. Prokic's family, many others and I all eat is yours too. As you can see, even the shoes and clothes that I wear are also yours. I immediately send everything that is extra to those who need it. I include monetary help as well. But I advise you to avoid asking me for money, for that is quite dangerous.

If I offer to lend you some, accept it. But it is better not to ask for it. Why? Because in doing so, you would be choosing the material path, but I am here to give you what you need for your spirit. My work gives food to your spirit, and in another way—for concerns of a material nature—I offer guidance so you can earn these things for yourself. People exist in order to work and create. After being born, we start immediately with our parents taking care of us. Later on, it is the educational institutions: schools, colleges and universities. After that, we apply the knowledge that we have gained there, and according to the results of our work, we earn money with which we buy the things that we need for living.

In the beginning, the path is painstaking and hard. This is God testing you to see how and in what way you will live and spend what you have earned. However, don't forget that negative energy is always present and is trying to get your attention and trying to mislead you from God's path.

In the beginning, you work hard and earn a little, but enough to be satisfied. But soon, a better job offer appears, when someone tells you that you can earn more with much less work. In these instances, greed awakens within you, and you start following this new route. You forget that God is always your companion.

In the beginning you might say: "Oh, God, if I only could earn enough for the apartment, the food and utilities. I only want good health and nothing more."

But after that better job offer appears, you suddenly want more and more. You are no longer satisfied with taking public transportation, but instead you dream of owning your own car. If you smoke, you are no longer satisfied with your old brand of cigarettes, but long for a better, more expensive brand. The negative energy is offering all of this to you. You somehow feel powerful and self-confident, and think that no one can do you any harm. The people in your environment start realizing that you are changing. You devote less and less attention to your spouse and your children at home. Then, you have affairs. You ignore God more and more, because now you are mimicking and acting like God. Completely oblivious, you remain unaware that you now already have one foot in hell, out of which, the way is very long and painful. You do not know that the maximum time period in which you can enjoy the fruits of somebody else's work is up to between five and seven years. After that, you pull your generation and yourself down.

I will give an example to help explain this. Let's suppose there is a married man who has worked very hard for the last 10 years and has saved $10,000. He lives with his wife and two children in a two-bedroom apartment. Suddenly, someone appears and asks this man to lend his money to them at a monthly interest rate of 10 percent. On the surface, it appears that this married man will receive $1,000 every month. This means that he would earn $10,000 in only 10 months, when it had originally taken him 10 years to save this amount.

I know that the majority of you have heard about similar situations, and some of you have even fallen for this same trap. People, as they are today, easily give their hard-earned savings away.

In the first two to three months, everything is all right and the married man receives a high monthly earning. Yet wanting more and more, he borrows another $20,000 from his family or friends, desiring to become rich overnight. He gives that money to the same person he lent his hard-earned savings to. In return, the married man receives a piece of paper stating that this particular person has borrowed a specific amount from him, and that he will be paid back the amount with interest after a specific number of months. The man is not aware that this person has not only taken money from him, but also from many others as well. And when the man comes to collect his interest payment, suddenly this person has excuses and says that he is not able to pay back the interest that day, but instead telling him to come back in a couple of days.

Still unsuspecting, the married man doesn't know that this person has collected many hundreds of thousands of dollars and is just about to flee.

Later, when the married man knocks on the door again, he finds himself standing there along with 10 other people in the same situation. He starts to panic and goes to a lawyer; but he doesn't realize that the lawyer is only going to take his money as well, because it is almost impossible to find the person who has fled. And the man has not only ended up without his $10,000 dollars, but he is now also indebted for another $20,000 dollars.

I personally do not feel sorry for these kinds of people, because they themselves created such a situation. Nobody forced them to do this; it was their own choice to give away their money.

And when they chose this way, they forget about God. The route out of this is very difficult, and one through which family members often suffer, as the parent's debt is transferred to his children.

For this reason, don't be greedy and long for more and more—because easy come, easy go.

10

SUCCESS OR FAILURE

Many times I have asked myself: What does it mean to succeed in life? Does it mean to be happy or to have money, a partner, marriage or children? Even today I am not sure, but I believe it means to be loved. When I talk of love, I am not only referring to the love we feel when we fall in love—rather, it is something we simply feel inside. To love means to not wish anything bad upon anyone else, to help others in trouble, to not cheat on your partner, and to not have an addiction to any material things.

Personally, I don't want to say anything about myself. I prefer to leave that to others. I often remember Ivica's words: "Braco, do not praise yourself. Leave that to others. Don't imagine how you want things to be, for we are only matter. Be guided by spirit." At the time, I didn't understand what Ivica meant. And now that I understand everything better, I would love to be able to let our dear Ivica know.

How I would love to take a drive with him again along our old routes, and maybe even argue a little with him because of my foolishness. He would give up on me many times, because he considered me a playful child I think. I can tell you now that I miss him very much. I sometimes retreat into myself. I think about him. I remember every moment spent with him, and it comforts me to know that someday we will be together again. But until then, I have much to do, this is only an intermediary stage compared to what awaits us.

During this last year I wrote a book entitled, *The Awakening.* I also published three videotapes under the same name, and another one called, *Braco.* I will let you determine whether all of these are a success or not. For me, personally, they are not, because in my view to succeed in life means to be happy. I will be happy the same day that the stain is removed from Ivica's name. The majority of you know that the press insulted Ivica in the last couple of months. The moment that people realize that he wasn't a black magician, some old fortune-teller, a Serbian "Chetnik" or who knows what else, I will be happy. Until then, I will fight and try to help you as much as I am allowed to. Understand, the moment you step in front of me, it will be decided how and in what way you will be helped. I only forward on your wishes—your prayers. Sometimes I pretend not to know anything. If help is given to you or not, I don't know up until the moment that you return and I see you in front of me again. I try to awaken your spiritual guide and send your guardian angel to protect you. That is all I can tell you for now. The rest depends on you.

The moment you get this book, which I have dedicated to you, you are instantly bringing Ivica and myself directly into your home. Sometimes a threatening reaction can arise from your family members, for it is difficult to find a family where everyone believes in such things. I understand and don't judge. Nowadays a lot of people are doing similar work, but are taking advantage of your weakness, sadness, pain and suffering instead. Their measure of success in giving help is for you to determine for yourselves. It is understandable that you may go once or twice, and if you see that nothing has changed, you won't go anymore. It's similar with me. When someone comes to me for the first time, I always give that person a book. Many ask themselves why I don't charge for it. It is because I don't have the right to do so. If that person has felt an improvement, then the next time he comes he can buy other books. This means that you evaluate me, and I prefer this. We will see if your improvements will continue or if they will fail.

Once a month I go with my colleagues from Srebrnjak 1 to Germany, where people also await my arrival eagerly. The crowd of followers is growing. Just a couple of days ago, some of the books'

German translations were published, but understand that I am not involved in this process. My aim is to try to make sure that positive energy is created around you, which will prevent the coming of the negative—the entry of negative deceased souls. Nowadays this is very hard, because the situation that humanity is in right now is unenviable. But whatever has occurred corresponds to the prophecy, which will have to be fulfilled. We shall see what will happen after that.

I suspect that I will be insulted publicly soon, because in the same way that I will become stronger, those who want to eliminate me will also gain strength. The press and media will attack me. Why? It is because many will not like the fact that you are coming here to Srebrnjak 1. They will try to destroy me—and this place. I don't know if they will succeed. Even though I know what awaits me, I will stand firm for as long as you continue to come here. I have nothing to lose. This is the path that I have chosen, and on which I will stay.

Time will tell if my force will become stronger or weaker. Surely you are wondering what this force is. It is you. You who come every day in growing crowds. Why? That's what I should be asking you.

11

LOVE

Love is the line between dream and reality; it is a line that each one of us desires to have, at least briefly in our lives. Unfortunately, in order to find love, there has to be much suffering. No one has successfully defined how we each can find it in our own way. Why? Because love is around all of us within our reach, but people today are looking for it somewhere else. Some believe that they have to sacrifice themselves for love; others believe that it is necessary to give it. However, it is here; it just has to be taken. How do we take it? Simply. One only needs to think of something nice and love is here. It comes instantly and slowly enters into us. Don't forget it will remain there as along as we deserve its presence. This means that the moment we think of something negative, love leaves, as this line is crossed—as when we think that someone doesn't love us or that everyone else is more useful, more beautiful and more deserving than us. We do not realize that beauty is created over years and decades, for love is that which creates it.

When we hear the word *love*, we immediately think of a girlfriend or boyfriend, but this is only a small part of love, like a drop in the ocean. Love comes slowly—similar to the way a bee approaches a flower. If we scare it, the bee will flee. Love will also flee. Love is creating in the same way a bee produces honey. You may ask what it is creating. It is creating a new life. Understand that a new life can also be conceived without love. Of course it can, but perhaps only after one, two, five or ten years will you realize that the fruit that has been created is nothing like what you wanted. Why? Because it had been created without love.

Whatever we do, without love it will not succeed.

You will realize that when a housewife and a baker bake bread, the bread is different even though they both used the same recipe and the same ingredients. However, the bread is not the same. Why? Often the baker is baking because he has to, and the housewife is baking it with happiness for her family or guests. Therefore, the difference is if you are doing something because you love to do it or if you're doing something because you have to.

This occurs in a similar way between a boyfriend and girlfriend. If you plan or if you want to show your friends that you can seduce a particular person, be advised that this relationship will break apart sooner or later. Why? It is because you have done this because of others. You were acting. There is no such thing as acting in love. Love cannot be touched; it has to be felt. It cannot be seen, but we can hear and smell it. Most of you know that each individual has his own specific smell. That's the way a dog is able to recognize his owner in a crowd of others.

This means that after you have spent a certain amount of time with your loved one, and after saying good-bye at the end of the day or night, you will still be smelling the scent of that person in your home. Even though that person is not physically with you, he or she is still there in a spiritual way.

And how long does love last? Today unfortunately it is short-lived. Apparently, being modern means having lots of boyfriends or girlfriends over the course of time. It seems this standard belief brings you more acceptance in society, but you forget that this is how seconds, minutes, hours, days, months and years pass. Life is a time in which we get older with every second, and every one of these seconds cannot be won back. One day when we get old, we look at the path we walked with several different partners, and we see that young people are doing the same. That's when we realize that we made a mistake, and that time has run out on us. In those moments we would like to give advice to those young people, but they would say: "Go away, old man. What do you know?"

Whenever our grandparents wanted to warn us about our mistakes, we used to say the same to them. Back then, we were young and hopeful, but we didn't realize that in time we would also grow old and that everything comes full circle one day. For this reason, don't look for love. Don't dream about it, but just take it—for it is there all around you. It's enough to think about love and it will come, but don't think with your brain, think with your heart. Love is not like mathematics, it cannot be calculated.

Act as it comes to you. Do not plan love; instead let it plan you. We are the ones who came from love, and this means that love created us, and not the other way around. For this reason, people, love each other; love with your heart, with your soul. Don't give importance to who you are, where you are from, who your father is or what your profession is. Let your heart guide you. Everything else is secondary, something you can think about in its own time.

If you interrupt this line between dream and reality, then only the dream remains. For a dream is one thing, and reality is another thing. No matter how much you would like to recreate this line, you will hardly succeed, because in life, you can only love once if you are lucky. Everything else becomes memories.

Therefore, try to love everyone. First love others, and then yourself, so that others will love you as well.

12

ARE WARS NECESSARY?

I have been asking myself for a long time: Why are there wars when they are unnecessary? However, they are inevitable. Why? Because wars control the number of inhabitants on Earth. The same goes for epidemic diseases. If we look at this more closely, we will realize that every century has had an incurable disease from which people have died. Yes, this is true. Science would find a medicine to cure a disease, and a new one would appear. Those from the past are cholera, typhus, and the plague. Today, there is AIDS, and soon there will be more. It sounds tragic, but it is true. This is a natural process through which the Earth's population is being regulated. If you take a close look at history, you will realize that wars have been occurring at least once a century. This happens for the same reason as epidemic diseases do. The biggest and most frequent warring conflicts occur in Europe, because that's where the majority of the countries are, and each of them wants the others to live and work according to their own rules. The only continent that was spared more or less from wars in the past is Australia. This is because God is protecting that territory because of a big secret it holds. I know that you now have a strong interest in this topic, but the time has not come yet to talk about this more.

This means that on one hand humanity is being created, and on the other it is being destroyed. This is the law of nature. The same goes for the world of animals. There are different types of animals, herbivores and carnivores, which take care of regulating the Earth's flora and fauna. The smaller birds exist in order to regulate the world of the insects. If the smaller birds did not exist, the insects would threaten us. The bigger birds of prey, such as falcons, hawks and eagles, regulate the numbers of smaller birds. Nature itself takes care of the number of the birds of prey; those birds hatch only rarely and in small numbers.

I would say that the wars are inevitable for now because this is a prophecy that had been given almost 2,000 years ago by the great and glorious Jesus Christ: "God forgive them for they don't know what they are doing. I am leaving now and taking all the sins from this world." We human beings did not understand what this meant, and put him on the cross. He said that he was leaving, but that he was going to come back after 2,000 years. This day is just about to come. What will happen after that, we will *find out?*

A lot of people ask themselves if is it possible to stop wars. I would say yes, it is. But understand that this is a time when certain countries want to have the predominant authority; they want to dominate other countries. As long as this view prevails, as long as people don't unite, as long as they don't realize that the borders between the countries are unnecessary and as long as they don't stop mimicking God, there will be wars. Something would have to happen so that people would start believing in God.

13

THE SUN

Now I will explain why this part of the book is called *The Sun*.

You might be wondering if I knew beforehand that it was going to be so named. Yes, I knew. If you have read the previous part, *The Awakening*, with attention, then you might have concluded that I was foreseeing a subsequent part. Let's start from the beginning. There is nothing more beautiful than to wake up in the morning and see the rays of the Sun through the window of one's bedroom. So, after the awakening, comes the Sun. It is that symbol that makes us happy. The moment we feel the rays of the Sun on our face, we simply feel happier and more cheerful. This is Father Creator himself wishing us a good morning and a successful day.

The Sun was created in the spring when nature

awakens. I would recommend that you bring warmth and happiness directly into your home with this part of the book, for the Sun determines everything. It determines if the year is going to be fertile or not. How? If the Sun shines too much, droughts will occur and harvests will be poor. If there is too much rain, there will be too much humidity and many floods. For this reason, it is necessary to establish a balance in order for humanity to be maintained.

We know that everything had been determined at the creation of this world, the same way God created four seasons: spring, summer, fall and winter. Each season has its own unique time period. This is neither too short, nor too long, but just as long as necessary. Even though science and technology have improved immensely, they still have not been able to influence the change of the seasons and the weather. Why? Because the ability to do so has not been given to them. We continue to try to invent spaceships in order to explore space. It sounds funny, since we still have not fully explored our planet. Billions of dollars are spent for the construction of these spaceships, and meanwhile, many people are dying of hunger. Why isn't this money being used, for example, to irrigate dried-out territories in Africa—which would be advantageous for all of us? Instead, some individuals seek fame in the annals of history, but so far this has not really improved anything for the rest of mankind.

Why has science not been able to prove the possibility of giving birth to two children who are exactly the same, or of the existence of two identical flowers?

Scientists try to prove that the Earth was created using their accepted scientific methods, but they don't understand that every living being possesses a spark, which is called *soul*. The moment the soul leaves the body, only matter remains, which then decomposes and goes back into Mother Earth from where it came.

So it is with the human body; it is like wearing a coat or pants. You will wear that piece of clothing until it is worn out, and then you will obtain a new one. That's the equivalent to how our spirit uses our body for as long as it is suitable. After that, it leaves the old body and enters a new one. We call this process death. In the astral world, however, death does not exist, but only eternity. It's also similar with the plants and the animals. Here on Earth everything is also regulated and planned beforehand. Flora awakens in spring when the Sun fertilizes it with his rays. However, the time span that the spirit lives in these plants is much shorter. This means that the Sun is that mechanism which starts and determines everything, which warms Mother God, but not all 24 hours per day. Why? She needs rest. That's why God created the night, for this is the state in which Mother Earth, as well as humanity, rests.

That sounds simple, doesn't it? It actually is. But today we have made our own lives more complicated.

14

GERMAN TOUR

In June 1995, a month after the tragic event, I traveled with my colleagues to Germany to try to explain to everyone there waiting for Ivica what had occurred. You can imagine how I felt. First of all, to express what had taken place was very hard for me. I just clenched my teeth and spoke with tears in my eyes. After that I asked myself, *What now?* I didn't know if I should work or not. Many people didn't believe what I had to say. A considerable number of people didn't believe me, for they were accustomed to working with Ivica. The best thing that could happen, I thought, was for me to be swallowed up by the Earth and disappear. So, what next? I pressed my teeth together and started working. As the people were approaching me one by one, I saw that many did not believe in me. I pretended not to notice any of it. About 70 people came that day. I was immediately told that half of them would give up and not return. I asked myself how I would work the next time. I received an answer saying that this was none of my business, and that I should work and not worry about the people.

A tour visit was held in the little city of Ludwigsburg, a suburb of Stuttgart. It was the first time we were going there, with the help of Zdenka, who had made an agreement with a restaurant owner to allow us to work in that location. I want to thank Zdenka, as well as Vlada and his wife, Josipa, who welcomed us without question or thinking it over. I realized immediately they were soon going to become true believers, even though they didn't know anything about Ivica or myself. I thank them from the bottom of my heart. That's when I decided not to change this event location going forward. The followers who had come with me agreed. (Now, there are always a couple of hundred people awaiting us at this place, so over time, success has come.) There was nothing to dread here, because the people coming were mainly new followers who had accepted my way of working. I had to speak with haste, since many people came just for the one day we were there to work.

Speaking of old followers who continue in their support, I would like to mention Mato, from Switzerland, who always gathers and invites more and more new people to come. I want to thank Mato with all my heart, because he is this link that connects Switzerland and our path. There is also Pero and his wife, Marta. Another person is Dragan, who is also from Switzerland and who not only visits us in Germany, but also visits us once a month in Zagreb. This is the path; you are the strength that holds me up. As long as you are here, I will be here too. Once the books had been translated into German, this signaled that the number of German followers was going to increase progressively. Now, there is already a decent number. If you ask me if I'm satisfied, I would answer yes. I think that we become stronger every day and, thereby, follow the path of Mr. Prokic.

Of course, there is Zora and her husband, Vlada. All of this would be hard to imagine without her, since she is the one who receives people's messages and calls and sometimes gives them a comforting word. Ivica chose Zora to be the one to plan and organize our visits in Germany. I want to use this opportunity to thank her, for she has never doubted in me or in my strength. I would need much more space in order to be able to thank each and every person. For this reason, I am now thanking everyone together for everything they have done for us in order to keep our visits happening abroad. Soon, I will have a new videotape filmed, not at Srebrnjak 1 in Zagreb, but in Germany. Then people in Croatia can view recordings of German events— in the same way Croatian events are now viewed in Germany.

Such is our work in Germany. Many people are

asking me if there will be any tours in other countries as well. I would say yes, as long as you want them. Meaning that I will go to places where people invite me to come.

15

FLOWERS

All of you are now familiar with my arrival at Srebrnjak 1, but you may not know how I spent my time in close proximity to Mr. Prokic. After my arrival, those first days consisted of sitting, listening and observing the ways of Ivica's work. I would sit the whole day without saying anything. There were moments when Ivica looked at me sideways, not saying anything, and I was afraid to move. I felt a bit bizarre, but calm. Neither did I dare to get up and go to the restroom, until Ivica would say, "Go pee boy, so you don't wet your pants here." I quaked and I left.

At that moment I thought: *Oh my God, he knows everything. It's not possible to lie to him.* I listened to everything, from confessions to lamentations and people's illnesses. Sometimes I looked at Ivica's old mirror, in the hope I would see something as well. But the only thing I saw was myself. I tried to concentrate better, but nothing happened. That's when Ivica looked at me and said: "Do not fool around, boy. It still has not been given to you. The time will come when you will be fed up with everything." So things have transpired, and this prophecy from Mr. Prokic was fulfilled.

I watched as some people brought in flowers. At that time, I thought that men only gave flowers to women, and I asked myself, *why they were bringing them here*? All of you may know that nowadays our center at Srebrnjak 1 is filled with flowers. Some people even bring a couple of bouquets. Yet, many of you are interested in knowing what purpose the many flowers serve, and I would like to explain this in more detail for you. It's with the help of these flowers that you are being healed. How? You know that flowers have pollen. With the help of this pollen, your guardian angel accompanies you; that is, I awaken him in order to accompany you. Because at times, the negative energy succeeds in putting your guardian angel to sleep, and that's why you feel sickness, have insomnia and get night sweats.

Simply speaking, your organism is blocked, as there is no guardian to protect you. When you come to see me, I try to awaken your angel, and after your visit at Srebrnjak 1, you feel happier, more cheerful and brighter. I fill you with a certain kind of energy, and your angel protects you. However, do not think that bringing flowers is necessary. Many times I hear people who come for the first time apologizing for not bringing flowers. I then tell them that this is not necessary, for people bring them in gratitude, but only after having received help.

16

MY WORK

I know that many of you are interested in knowing about how I work, and how you are being helped. First of all, this is something that one cannot learn, for someone can only receive it.

About a month ago, a young man in his early twenties came to see me, and told me that he would like to be liberated from his body so that he could fly like a bird. I immediately asked myself if I should receive him or tell him to leave. I was told to let him speak. I saw that he had many unusual wishes stemming from psychological problems. He had not accomplished anything in life; his parents were supporting him while he was imagining himself to have special powers. I asked him who had told him about me. And he answered that people were talking a lot about my work, saying that I could help with many issues.

I told him that this was true, but that I couldn't fulfill his wish, for one must have wings in order to fly. Due to the fact that he was a human like me, I couldn't help him. I told him that I didn't have the power he thought I had, and that I didn't know anyone personally who could help him to fulfill his wish. The young man was surprised, because he was expecting me to tell him stories of others who knew such things. He told me that he had read several books in the field of astrology, in diverse occult sciences and more. He was confused when I told him that I was not a big reader. He indeed thought that I had a collection of books to refer to, from which he could learn something. You must understand that what I have cannot be learned; one simply has to receive it as a gift.

Another case involved a mother, who came with a photo of her daughter and said that her daughter had been having serious nightmares for the past 10 days. As soon as she closed her eyes, she saw creatures that wanted to kill her. And she was endlessly falling into an abyss, and it simply wouldn't stop. I immediately asked the mother what her daughter did. She said that her daughter was a student and had started taking Reiki classes about a month before. I didn't know what Reiki was, but she informed me that it was some sort of relaxation technique that helps with resolving illnesses and provides increased energy. I immediately knew that the girl had made a mistake along the way, in that she had done the meditation in an incorrect manner that caused a counterproductive effect.

I told the mother to come back if she saw an improvement of her daughter's health in the next seven days.

And indeed, the day before yesterday, mother and daughter appeared at my door with two bouquets of flowers in order to thank me, because the daughter's health had improved. She was completely free of her previous problems. I touched her with my hand, and she said that she felt some warmth and happiness. This is exactly what I can give to you. If you think that you will see something—some kind of miracle, or something similar—you are mistaken. Understand that God's force cannot be seen; it simply has to be felt.

The material thing that I am giving to you is only a book, through which you bring me, as well as Mr. Prokic, into your home. There are videos as well, and they help you to visualize Mr. Prokic and me, along with the protective sign, the Sun symbol—which protects you. Success is most often achieved in cases involving the resolution of love problems, nightmares, the ability to create progeny, etc. But if you believe that it is enough to just come anytime to see me and that your problems will be resolved, then you are mistaken. I know that you don't understand this, but it is not important. Therefore, when you are driven by some positive energy, come. Do not come against your will, for that's when you cannot be helped. Do not convince others to come, because they will make fun of you, for the time is not yet right for them. Nothing can be sped up.

Be assured, the one who is destined to come will do so. In the beginning, I tried to convince many of my friends to come. I told them that there was a man, in Zagreb at Srebrnjak 1, who saw and knew everything, and could help at the same time. It was only necessary to believe, and help came on it's own. Even though Ivica told me to be quiet, to not talk publicly in this way, I didn't listen to him. During that time, everyone insulted me. But today, these same people, who once insulted me, are coming to see me the same way you are. I don't judge them, and I try to help them as I help you.

For this reason, don't try to convince anyone. Because as long as their spiritual guide is still sleeping, and until the light switch is pressed, the bulb doesn't illuminate and they cannot come. Let time take care of it. Those of you who are protecting me will do this best by not talking too much about all of this. Understand that the seagulls—the books—are still weak, and that in this moment a new one is being born, which will release thousands of new ones into the world.

So, be quiet and attend your own business every day, and keep in mind that our Ivica is around us in every moment. It is enough to just call him, and he will be there.

17

INDIA

After a break of about a month, here I am again. The writing of this book has been prolonged; the time period when you will read it is still undetermined. Even I, as the author, cannot write whenever I choose. So, here we are, again together on April 24, 1996. Exactly a year ago yesterday, April 23, we were separated physically from our beloved Ivica. I am aware that this is difficult for everyone. Yesterday plenty of people came here, not only from Zagreb, Croatia, but also from many other countries. It makes me happy that people came in such a large number, for this means that they are still following his path. Unfortunately, there are also a lot of people visiting who didn't have the chance to meet him personally. They can only see him in photos, the books and videos. So, all of you who follow his path without having personally met him, go to the Mirogoj Cemetery where his body rests and light a candle, for he is the founder and the initiator of all of this. Without him none of this would exist.

After I first arrived at Srebrnjak 1, Ivica used to tell me: "You see, Braco, life has given you everything. You have money, you could travel, and so you have traveled. But you did all of this just out of curiosity. The time will come when you will travel to many countries and continents. I know that you don't understand this now, but people will be longing for you." Back then, he talked about many countries and people, including Sai Baba, the famous miracle worker who had supernatural powers and could help people. The majority of you will have heard about him, and know that he was famous for possessing the power to materialize objects out of thin air.

It was because of this conversation that I later decided to visit Sai Baba at his ashram in India. I personally didn't know much about him, so I didn't have any particular opinion about him. Therefore, I wanted to go and find out more. I left with my friend Pero on January 17, 1996. Our stay in India was supposed to last one month. Our flight was quite tiring and took about 35 hours, because we didn't have a direct flight and had to change planes a couple of times. After our arrival and an overnight stay in Bangalore, India, we traveled at dawn by taxi to Puttaparthi, where Sai Baba's ashram was. The air there was dry without humidity, and the temperature was about 27 degrees Celsius (81 degrees Fahrenheit). When we left Zagreb, it was 0 degrees Celsius (32 degrees Fahrenheit). So, it was quite a sudden change to experience in less than two days.

After a six-hour taxi drive, we arrived at Sai Baba's Puttaparthi ashram. Lodging for the night cost less than a dollar per person for those with little economic means, and for those with more, three dollars per person. After we had reserved a room, which consisted of one bed and a sink with a tap, I realized that the hygienic conditions were minimal. However, I had a strange desire to meet this man. Yet at the same time I felt restless inside; I wanted to stay and leave at the same time. Suddenly, I remembered the Community of Srebrnjak 1, and I felt a huge nostalgia for everyone.

We rested a little bit in our room after checking in at the reception center, as every day at 4 p.m. Sai Baba made an appearance. His ashram looked like a huge complex from the inside, and I had never seen anything like it before, not even on television. It was built in a special style, really fascinating for the eye to behold. However, since one could not enter in normal attire, we had to buy specific linen shirts and pants so that we were dressed the same as everyone else. Taking off one's shoes before entering was mandatory. Everyone had to be barefoot. I was a little bit surprised that such strict rules existed. Smoking was forbidden as well. I knew that Pero was a passionate smoker, but I told him that he had to hang on. I saw that there were metal detectors at the door, for checking if someone was carrying weapons or not. Approximately 300 meters from the entrance, we came to the main hall, where thousands of people had come together, most of them kneeling and praying. It was 3:45 p.m.

I knew that we were going to see Sai Baba soon. Indian music gently sounded, and after it ended, the movable ceiling was opened and the view was astonishing.

That's when he appeared, dressed in an orange robe with a smile on his face. He started walking down the rows of people. He walked slowly, which looked unnatural, as if he were floating. He was short, about 1.6 meters (5 feet 3 inches). I was expecting him to say something, however, he didn't utter a word. He walked in a circle once, twice, and then left. At one side of the hall were seriously ill people, cripples, invalids and blind people. He only looked at them and passed by.

If you ask me if I felt something, I would say yes, some strange flow through my body.

Many people have called him a swindler or a thief, but I would not agree. First of all, if he were a swindler, he wouldn't have been able to gather such great crowds of people together. According to the number of followers he has, I would say that he is the strongest of all in this regard. I asked how he was able to materialize things. I was told that he simply entered another dimension, another time. I believe he is from another planet, from another God. You will not understand this for now, but I will explain it later.

The whole ritual lasted about 20 minutes, and then he left, only to return the next day at dawn. He appeared twice each day, at 6 a.m. and at 4 p.m. I was told that if one spends about 30 days at the ashram, there might be a possibility to talk to him in person and to be told something about oneself. I was heavily debating staying or going back. Pero and I stayed one night, and I decided the next morning to go back to Zagreb. But this wasn't easy, because our return tickets were booked for the next month. I asked around if there was any possibility to change our tickets. I was told that we had to wait a couple of days. "A couple of days?" I said, "I need to go back today." Suddenly an even a bigger desire to go home overcame me. I knew I had seen that what I had come for. I thought about resting a little bit and discovering India, however, the pull of the Community of Srebrnjak 1 was stronger. Your desire for my return was stronger, and I decided to come back as soon as possible. I looked at Pero, he only smiled, and I realized that he was longing for Zagreb in the same way I was.

I found some man and asked him if he could help us with our return. He looked at me in a strange way and told me that I seemed honest to him, and he assured me personally of our return. After he had made a couple of phone calls, he told me that we would be flying back to Europe the same day at 4 p.m. He said that we had to give him our passports

123

and that he would send his driver from Bangalore to pick up our tickets. At first I was a little scared, because I was aware that once I gave him our passports, we would be left without proper documents. God forbid if something happened—we would have serious problems trying to return to our country. I was gambling on everything or nothing. So, I gave him our passports. We had to wait a couple of hours until we were told that the tickets had been purchased. And the same day at 4 o'clock we found ourselves at the airport. As we did not inform anyone at Srebrnjak 1 of our spontaneous return, there was no end to the surprise when we got home.

I'm sure you will all be interested in knowing something more about Sai Baba. I think he is someone with great abilities, and whom people in India perceive as a saint. I talked with many people about him while we were there, and everyone thought of him like a deity, not like a human being. I didn't see anything negative. I was surprised to see such security and armed bodyguards around him. In one way, it is quite understandable, because incredibly large numbers of people come to see him.

In the end, I would say that people have to be their own judge. It was surely beautiful to have observed everything, but the question if he is going to help you—one has to feel that for oneself. And if you think it helped, go again.

I personally went there for only one reason: because I had talked to Ivica about him.

18

THE FUTURE

I know that everyone has an interest in knowing what the future will bring. The time ahead is an unknown for both scientists and all human beings. Many people have tried to use various methods to figure out something more about their own futures, or about the future in general. Today, at the end of the 20th century, humanity has achieved great advances in technology. It has built superfast luxurious planes, boats and cars. However, if we take a look at the past, we will notice that the most significant achievements have been made in this century after World War II, particularly in the last 50 years. Today it seems like we know everything. It becomes apparent as we look around that the cities are overcrowded, and meanwhile the villages are becoming smaller and smaller in population.

Everyone is longing for a life in the big cities, for people are unaware that life there is much harder than in the countryside. Everyone wants the life of a gentleman, but they forget that they have mainly descended from farmers. The time we live in is a strange one, and the majority of us are sick of this form of living where it seems like everything is planned.

All of us know in what way we will spend our time day to day. However, there is a desire in everyone of us to know more about the overall future, for everyone feels that something important is going to happen. Yes, I, like you, also feel that changes are coming. Catastrophes are going to happen. I see some strong earthquakes and wars between the superpowers. I don't have the right for now to name these countries. I see that some institutions will progressively loose their reputations, but this will be their own fault, for they can trick people only as long as it has been determined. There will be heavy droughts too.

I do not perceive this as the end of the world as many have thought. The truth is that many will die, but after that, a golden era will come for those remaining. It will be a time with no differences between nations or religions. We will realize that we are all equal, and that we have all been created by the same God. We have to comprehend that material things are temporary, and that they all have a limited lifetime. Understand that in the moment we are born, our spirit simply enters this suit of armor, which is our physical body, and remains there as long as it needs it. The moment our body is used up, the spirit abandons it. Now, in this life, you are a man, in the next a woman, in this one white and in the next one black. The spirit has been given the opportunity to reincarnate seven times, which means that spirit can change the body this many times. Afterwards, one remains only a spirit who is wandering and traveling in eternity. For now, this is not comprehended, but the time will come when it will be.

At times when we sleep and, in turn, dream, our spirit sometimes leaves the physical body and travels. That is the time when it is free and gets rest. Some feel delight, tiredness, happiness or sadness or experience night sweats,. It all depends on the path through which your spirit travels. After waking up, it is best not to remember anything, so that the things that you dreamed about won't bother you. However, the time in which we live is tumultuous, and the majority of us have nightmares and insomnia, and look even more tired after waking up than before going to bed. Therefore, try to bring a little joy and happiness into your life. Do not talk constantly about work, money and illnesses, for this only attracts negative energy. Laugh, because then something new will happen, something that will come quietly and slowly, and which will break the monotony and the fear around you. We are still weak at this moment. However, a strengthening is visible.

It is important that I am very careful with my

writing, for many will try to interpret the content in my book in the most diverse ways. Understand that I am still young. I do not refer only to age; however, I am probably the youngest of those who dedicate themselves to these things, but I refer to the time of creation. A whole year has still not passed, and more and more people come all the time. I have to be careful, because evil tongues are on the wait to see if I will write something in error, and therefore fall into their trap. I believe that I will preserve all of what I have been given, for I am proud that I had our beloved Ivica as a teacher. For this reason, I continue to walk on this path, the path of truth, and I will try to carry on this work with what has been given to me. But now, whenever you step in front of me, I speak less and less, because my words are being misinterpreted.

The moment I smile at you or touch you with my hand, I am giving you what you need. It is not necessary for me to talk to you about different things; this is not really what helps you anyway. You came here seeking help: joy, happiness and satisfaction. But as I have emphasized many times, understand that it is not enough to only come and see me, for you must also believe.

In the end, I would like to thank my Community, which didn't doubt in me for a second, but accepted me like Ivica. I know that I am not Ivica and I am not trying to be him. I am only trying to transmit to you that which has been given to me.

I would like to thank Ivica for having named me

his right hand, for having allowed me to be at his side in every moment and for having given me the opportunity to continue the path that he started and walked on.

Love, your Braco.

19

AT THE END OR AT THE BEGINNING

We are now at the conclusion of my book. If you ask me how I feel right now after finishing this work, I would say strange, the same way I felt at the very beginning.

Even though I cannot see our dear Ivica with my eyes, I don't feel his absence, for it's as though he is here by my side. I can feel, see and hear him, and I listen to his messages. I want you to understand that I have nothing at all to do with anything that is written here. Yet, I believe it won't be difficult for anyone to guess the key to everything. Yes, it is Ivica. Because his strength will remain to act upon me the same way it acts upon all of you. Just remember what Ivica used to say: "It is only necessary to believe, and help will come by itself."

I know that nowadays this sounds a little ridiculous, for we have learned to pay for everything with money. But there is no such thing here. For this reason some will just shake their head and say: "There is nothing to it. How will you get help if you don't pay for it and don't get anything visible in return?"

Those are the well-known temptations, which we have to pass like a test, since we have been given this whole life by God, and hence are being assessed by him.

The moment our candle of life extinguishes, the spirit leaves the body and becomes free. Actually, that is when everything begins. Up until then, we have only been slaves. Our body is like a suit of armor in which our spirit is tortured and suffers. After our spirit leaves our body, it is then judged for everything that its body did while on Earth, Mother God.

Mother God protects and takes care of our physical body, whereas, Father God does the same for our spirit. It is similar with human beings. The father of each child makes certain to teach him or her something, guiding the child to the right path of life and passing on his knowledge. The mother of each child takes care of his or her health, ensures that the child is dressed properly and that the child has eaten well.

I hope it is clear that just as Father God takes care of our spirit—and as Mother God, the Earth, takes care of our physical body—this same process occurs in a similar way within a family. This is the chain that we are part of, the chain that is impossible to tear apart. The negative energies will try to break this chain, but they will not succeed.

Here at the very end, I wish you much love, happiness, health and satisfaction. I will be available at Srebrnjak 1 for as long as you continue to wish it. The same is true for my colleagues.

I would like to take this chance to thank Mrs. Prokic on behalf of myself, as well as on your behalf, for understand that she is the one who gave us the opportunity to continue to gather together at Srebrnjak 1. I promised her that I would continue to take care of her, her son, Alen, and her daughter, Marjana. Know that after the great tragedy, difficult times occurred for her, and perhaps any other woman in her place would have done the opposite and locked up that space to keep the memories of her husband only for herself. However, she acted in a different way and conducted herself the way Mr. Prokic had described her. Once again, I thank her from the bottom of my heart.

I don't include Ivica here, for he is the crown, the crown of everything. He is the beginning and the end. He lasts in all of us, and we are here to protect, take care of and continue all that Ivica has created. We all carry a seed inside, which can become a beautiful fruit one day.

Your Braco loves you very much.

Epilogue

MY NEXT BOOK

This seems like a proper moment to tell you that I still feel a bit incomplete. Therefore, here at the end, I have tried to see my next book, and I was told that there will be a next book, but this depends solely on you. Over the last year of working, many of you have expressed the wish for your words of gratitude to appear in my book, but at the time I didn't know if that was going to be possible.

I was just told in this moment that the next book will be your book, and you will be the ones writing it. I will only convey your words. Therefore, all of you who have felt help in any way and all of you who wish this to be known in public, just write a letter—mail it, or bring it personally. This is that path. You are the strength that goes on, that spreads and continues the path, which Ivica created. We are actually only a mechanism that spreads the truth about him. If you would like others to know about this work, write about it. In the same way that these books heal, you will be strengthened and enabled to reach others. Know that your example can help others, because with the aid of your spiritual guide, you will be given the opportunity to help others. This book will not only be read by our generation, but also by many other generations to come. And it will not only be read in Croatia, but also in all other countries and continents in many languages.

May the Sun, which is our symbol, protect and warm us the way it warms Mother God, the Earth. May it create new followers, the same way it creates new life. May Ivica have eternal glory, and may he be proud of us.

Out of the many letters that I have received in the past year, I have selected this one along with some poems as a sample.

Dear Braco,
Even though the date on my book, June 7, 1995, is very fresh, even though I practically just came back from Srebrnjak 1, I can't resist the desire to write down the words in pencil, which simply need to come out of me. The whole day I have been resisting writing this letter, and finally lost the battle. Now it is night, past one a.m., and I am still fulfilled with some strange energy. I won't be able to get to sleep until I say what is in my heart. I want to apologize first, for I am allowing myself the impertinence of addressing someone whom I admire in

an informal way. But I simply cannot find the place in my thoughts to use "sir." When I think about the plural "you," I then think about both Ivica and Braco. That's why I will address you in an informal way, but not with less respect and admiration. I would also like to apologize for using this letter as means of expression, but I think if I came to Srebrnjak 1 and started talking about everything I wanted to express, there would be no time for anyone else. That's why I think that this is the best way. I am asking for your understanding, dear Braco, that the reason of my writing is much deeper and stronger than I can express with words.

Such strange but delightful things are happening inside of me, that I simply cannot manage all the stream of feelings that are overflowing in me. On June 7, 1995, I came the first time to Srebrnjak 1 since Ivica was gone. I didn't want to know what was going to happen tomorrow; I didn't want to know what destiny was holding. I only wanted a little support. Coming to Srebrnjak 1, sitting there and waiting for my opportunity, some strange excitement came over me. It was an unknown and unexplainable feeling in me. Not fear, not worry, not dread, but something unknown, unusual. When I entered the room where Ivica once sat, the room where I once was able to see him—I became convinced that he was still there—I started to stutter, and my voice was trembling. I said what I had to; I talked about a dream I had. I will never forget Ivica's words upon our first meeting: "You will dream, your dreams are telling you things. You will know everything." And then you gave me a book and told me that I was going to find all of my questions, along with the answers, in the book. You told me that once I read the book, something good would happen. And I felt that it was good, that I shall come again. Everything that I could say was so meager compared with what I owe you. Such a small thank-you. And yet that's where everything starts.

I am heading out, carrying the book in my hand, and it's as if I wasn't touching the ground. I am floating, because something warm, something that fulfills me completely flows through me. I am smiling, overjoyed, and I still don't know how to explain everything. I travel back to my house, singing and thinking. Overjoyed because of the feeling that I have, yet I am persecuted by a feeling of guilt. I feel pain. Braco, I feel your pain. I feel that you are doing all that you have to, but that the pain of Ivica's absence is choking you. "God forbid this happens to anyone," Ivica would say. What do you feel, and what are you fighting with? You know that best, and I would like to tell you that for what you're doing, you deserve more than any of us who come to see you. Nevertheless, you are giving us all that is sweet, and leaving bitter wormwood for yourself. I would like to let you know that we will justify all of Ivica's battles and the love he gave us. He simply became part of us. He lives in us, in our hearts and thoughts. We were worthless without him. Our souls were cripples, poor; we were mortals full of regret and sins. He changed everything. Life makes sense; life is worth living. No matter how difficult life is, it is fulfilled with such beauty, hope and faith. I know that Ivica is next to you and will never abandon you. I know that you are now his body, and even though you are a different person, he is inevitably part of you. Forgive me for directly stating these things; I hope that you will understand that I simply feel this way. I don't want to think that I am in error, because the moment I found out that Ivica died, I said: "We have Braco. He will work." I didn't cry, for Ivica had taught me that you don't cry for the deceased. It hurts, of course, but I found my consolation in prayer. It was worth it, believe me.

Reading his previous books, I realized in advance that it was actually you who would have to replace him. But because it happened so suddenly and tragically, it was frustrating. I was thinking a lot about how Ivica was living with the knowledge of what was going to happen. Only now do I see that he knew this too, and I always ask myself what would have happened if, by any chance, he had won this battle as well. He did win in, but in another way: by sacrificing himself and his family. What would have happened if he actually were physically with us? This question will obviously have to wait to be answered. But that's why I have to admit that I received many answers reading your books. Thank you for every written word, for every truth. Never have I ever read something as readable as this. I was receiving my answers almost telepathically. I was so often the renegade in society. Nowadays they still tell me that I'm crazy, that I live in the ethers, and not on the earth along with the cellar-like smell of the bars and the noise of drunken people. I am only looking for my peace, and that's why they consider me a freak. I spent hours and hours fishing, running away from the city, staring at the murky surface of the Drava River. Traveling with it, fearing it, but still closely approaching it. I've been running away from myself for days and years, because one part of me always knew that I was a sinner. That part always pushed me to look for something else, and not for the life that I was living. However, I was always coming back and sinning. Nonsense would come out of my mouth, my actions were disgusting, so that thinking about everything, I was repugnant to myself. And so, when the water came up to my throat, and when I couldn't go anywhere else, that's when I came to Ivica, all dirty and poor.

When I first saw his book that one of my friends had had since 1991, I told her: "There's nothing to it. Look at that gypsy. Stay away from him. How would you know that he isn't dealing with black magic?" Do you recognize these words? That same man didn't accuse me of anything, but on the contrary, started consoling and teaching me. I know that I still have to learn many, many things, and that there is still evil inside of me, but I believe that with my desire and faith along with your help, Braco, I will succeed. Never before have I felt real love. Not even in my family, because somehow I don't belong there. I got to know that unknown feeling for myself at Srebrnjak 1. I received love and nobody asked me to give it back in any way. I would be immensely happy if I knew that you also feel what you give to others, and I will pray to God to give you all the love you delivered to others—to return to you all the happiness you give others. I would like to come to Srebrnjak 1 and feel that you're happy, and see you smiling the same way Ivica always used to. I am grateful to God for giving you to us, especially now that we need you immensely. I will never forget Ivica's last words for me: "You don't know how many enemies you have. May all the Gods protect you on your path." I would like to say that you, Braco, don't know how many friends you have, and how happy those are who love you. I believe that you have understood what my scribbling is about, and I will finish writing, because I could go like this for hours.

I will look for the answers to all my questions in the books. I hope that I will soon come again, and bring away a book that I don't have yet.

Poem for Ivica and Braco

I only heard about you once
and felt invited the same instant.
I was in a part miserable state,
because the events that had to happen
were covered by a shadow of insecurity.

Not asking for the work commitments,
not fearing the nasty situation,
which could have been the result of my actions,
an energy brought me to you.
I admit, I could not hide the excitement.

I was walking in a room full of flowers
as if calmness was caressing me, a candle warming me.
I was floating with an invisible fluid, free like a bird.
It was an idyllic life story.

To expose my first problem,
which was causing disturbance in the blood.
And in a short time, a miracle happened,
because I felt I had been forgiven my sins.

"That's how it is!" To shout in myself
because my faith had brought about a fruit.
How I didn't doubt in any instant
to feel happiness under the firmament.

And for the second time
I was your guest in a strange way.

I asked for advice
about something I had been dreaming for a year.
You granted my wish
and to proceed how I wanted was easier.
To feel happiness again,
one must not renounce this, therefore I won't.

The verses are mine,
the biggest treasure I have created 'til today.
And there is a poem about them as well,
in which I talk about
what they mean to me.
That's why I am giving them to you,
so that pieces of my soul radiate
and accomplish the touch
with the very dear and holy place to me.

Happy and blessed Easter wishes,
Your Davor

To the Sun, Ivica and Braco

There's no more beautiful light
than yours
There's no warmer love
than yours
There's no stronger strength
than yours
There's no bigger sacrifice
than yours
There's no faster river
than yours
There's no more faithful shepherd
than you
There's no more fruitful grain
than yours
I know and am waiting
because I want you to come back
You are that light
new life
the path to eternity

April 23, 1996
D. P.

Srebrnjak 1

There's a beautiful holy place next to us,
where many people have found their soul's salvation.
That's where love, truth, happiness and joy are the
biggest treasure.
The one who gets there will be very happy.
That's where one acquires the most love and truth.
That's where one recognizes all of life's untruths.
One will get to know himself, he will get to know others
as well.
That's where one will solve all the life's pain and
sadness.
That's where the Sun is always shining,
warming all of us beautifully, tenderly.
That's where God's eye is accompanying us
and will lead us back to the right path.
To live with God's love is the biggest treasure of the
world,
everything is flourishing of happiness there.
Let's wake up, people, let's look for salvation,
there were only God's voice is heard.
God gave us also his son.
Let's accept, people, love and faith in God,
And his son he gave us,
to guide us into a better tomorrow, so that our tomorrows
will be sparkling.
He gave us everything, let's accept it, let's not let evil
prevail.
Let's fight, people, with love and truth, faith and smile,
and not with hate and sin.

Let's come people, come here, and we will fight with love...
Let's come here, we will feel the peace and serenity of our soul,
and evil will not choke us.
We will all be happy and cheerful, will smile happily forever.
Thank you very much for everything, dear God, Ivica and Braco.

For Ivica and Braco

With 28 summers, Guardian Angel.
Your soul is holy, you deserve God's glory.
You have done much, you will be doing much more,
for your people, for all of us, who
looked for our soul's salvation with you, Angel.
Our Angel, you are suffering a lot
to bring us all back to the right path.
My heart is singing, my soul exclaiming,
as I'm watching how life after life sprouts.
You are giving us happiness, saving marriages,
you remove darkness from our souls.
The light is shining for us, warming our soul,
Happiness is being born and our soul is younger and
younger.
You are guiding us to God and want to please everyone
But you've had only 28 summers, all the holy love is in
your heart.
We want to offer a huge thank-you
for everything that your hand has given us.
I would like to tell everyone, the whole world, about you,
but I'm afraid, our Angel, that they will besmirch you.
But time will come when I will be able
to say everything that my heart wants to say.
But my heart knows what the Lord's and your hand is
giving me.
Our savior has arrived, has risen his voice to the
heavens,
He told us: "I wish you much happiness. I only share
love, happiness, health and joy with you."

J. G. BRACO

Once again, a huge thank-you
for everything that your strength has given.

Braco Today ~ 2013

RESOURCES

Main Websites

USA: www.braco.net
Europe: www.braco-info.com
Russia: www.braco.ru

- *View the latest live event & live streaming schedules*
- *Sign up for the Braco e~Newsletter*

Live Streaming

Participate in a live stream Braco gazing session from anywhere in the world—using your computer or smart phone.

www.braco-tv.com

Braco Books, DVDs & CDs

USA: www.braco.net/dvds

Facebook.com

Braco & Ivica
Braco Australia

Made in the USA
Charleston, SC
11 June 2016